THE JACK SPRAT
COOKBOOK

THE JACK SPRAT COOKBOOK

Delicious Low-Fat Food

SCOTT EWING

GRAFTON BOOKS
A Division of the Collins Publishing Group

LONDON GLASGOW
TORONTO SYDNEY AUCKLAND

Grafton Books
A Division of the Collins Publishing Group
8 Grafton Street, London WIX 3LA

Published by Grafton Books 1986

British Library Cataloguing in Publication Data
Ewing, Scott
The Jack Sprat cookbook: delicious low-
fat food.
I. Low-fat diet – Recipes
I. Title
641.5'638   RM237.7

ISBN 0-246-12765-1

Photoset by Rowland Phototypesetting Ltd,
Bury St Edmunds, Suffolk
Printed in Great Britain by
William Collins Sons & Co. Ltd, Glasgow

Jack Sprat could eat no fat,
His wife could eat no lean,
And so between them both, you see,
They licked the platter clean.

For my father

CONTENTS

ACKNOWLEDGEMENTS

Trying to thank everyone who has helped bring this book to life is a task almost as difficult as writing it. One's ideas and insights are shaped over many years by family, friends and colleagues. Of these I am especially indebted to Mary Shepherd, Renée Sproull, Keith Botsford, Gretel Beer, Elisabeth Lambert Ortiz and Phyllis Naylor as well as Patti Langton, Rosamond Man, Elisabeth Longley, Lee Faber and Leslie Elliott.

For practical assistance my sincere gratitude goes to Joey Chapter for typing the manuscript and again to Rosamond Man for invaluable advice, encouragement and support during many long and often late-night conversations. Well-earned praise and thanks are due to my ever-helpful greengrocers Roger, Kevin and Ken at Southside Fruiterers, and Danny and Gary at Moen Butchers in Clapham Common. Special recognition, too, for Jane and Lynn Wells, Mr and Mrs John Edwards, Debra Botwood, Bob Purdom and Marie-Pierre Moine who helped me taste, evaluate and enjoy many of the recipes.

INTRODUCTION

Sacrifice is not one of my strong points, but when doctors asked me to give up a rich diet in order to look and feel well, I decided to try. They persuaded me that by substantially reducing the amount of fat I ate and avoiding rich foods, the heaviness, and often sickness, that I felt after meals would disappear. They were right. Lack of energy, rashes and other skin complaints also improved dramatically. I was then a university student with my own digs, so cooking for myself was easy, but whenever I over-indulged in fatty foods, the problems recurred. Occasional lapses were good for my education as they quickly reminded me of my limits.

Exploring the world of low-fat cookery was fascinating. Cooking had been a major interest since childhood and I had just returned to America from a year in Europe, where I'd been exposed to the glories of French cuisine and had worked with Swiss chefs in a restaurant in Chelsea. I was also pining for my grandmother's Southern cooking with its fried chicken, steaks with cream gravies, vegetables and hot bread dripping with butter, pies and cakes. So, I began to develop low-fat versions of my favourite dishes and to create others using healthier, less rich ingredients. Even when entertaining friends, it was perfectly possible to prepare full-flavoured, satisfying meals without any palate-troubling sense of compromise or deprivation.

That was a decade ago; now as a cookery writer and editor, food is my profession. My life revolves around healthy food and fitness, so I welcome the increasing media coverage about the importance of healthy eating. The more publicity there is, the easier it is to persuade friends that my style of cooking will actually improve their health, especially those who have suddenly been confronted by a doctor's decree that they, or the person for whom they cook, must radically reduce the fat, salt and often sugar in their diet.

Medical and scientific research in the last 20 years has come to show beyond reasonable doubt that the diet most people eat in modern, industrialized nations is the main single underlying cause of disease. What we eat can greatly increase our chances of suffering, and dying, from heart disease, strokes or cancer. These three illnesses jointly kill two out of every three people and the research also strongly links diet to diabetes, gallstones, obesity and constipation. By the age of 40, the majority of people in Britain suffer from at least one of these complaints, and often several.

So what is this deadly diet? A UK report by the National Advisory Committee on Nutrition Education (NACNE) concluded that it contains too much fat, particularly saturated fat. This comes mainly from meat and dairy products, and is often 'hidden' in sausages, crisps, ice cream, candy bars and other processed convenience foods. In order to cut down on total fat, it's best to choose foods that have a lower fat content. For instance, fats that are solid at room temperature such as butter, lard, suet and the fat on meat have a high level of saturated fat. Less saturated fats are found in vegetable oils, and in some soft margarines made from them. Chicken, turkey, rabbit, and oily fish such as mackerel and herring, have less saturated fat in them than beef, lamb and pork have. The NACNE experts recommend that only about 35 per cent of one's total food energy (calories) should come from fat, and only 14 per cent of this should be saturated fat. To put it more simply, the average person should cut back on the total amount of fat they eat, reduce the amount of saturated fat by one quarter, and eat more starches and whole grain cereals, vegetables and fruit.

But low fat doesn't mean no fat. Fat makes food taste good and some fat in our food is essential to good health. The fat we normally eat provides us with compounds such as linoleic acid which prevents drying and flaking of the skin, and helps maintain proper growth in children. The fatty compounds also help to create certain substances needed for various body processes. As our bodies can't make these compounds, we have to get them from our food. Even people on a severely fat-restricted diet should, according to nutritional experts, get at least 25 per cent of their daily calories from fats. Meals low in fat can leave a person feeling hungry, because fats are digested slowly and so keep hunger from recurring too soon. People often complain of hunger soon after eating Chinese food, probably because the dishes they ate consisted mainly of vegetables with a high moisture content, and only small amounts of poultry or meat. This would not be the case after eating even the leanest fillet steak, because the lean meat itself contains some fat and *very* delicious it is, too!

Many people are confused about cholesterol, a fatty substance vital for human cells and tissues and for making certain hormones. Cholesterol is produced in the liver where it is broken down into bile acids which aid proper digestion. All body cells can make their own cholesterol. Cells, however, are more likely to take what they require from the bloodstream. This cholesterol comes from digested animal foods as well as some fish and shellfish, though plant foods contain none.

When the body has enough cholesterol, the cells no longer take it from the bloodstream, and the unabsorbed cholesterol can be measured by doctors. Their studies show that the more cholesterol-rich foods we eat, the higher the cholesterol that can be measured in our blood. Too much circulating through the bloodstream causes fatty deposits, which cling to artery walls. Over time, with continuing high amounts of cholesterol in the blood, these deposits increase in size and can cause circulation problems – and eventually heart attacks. (Fortunately the studies also show that eating less cholesterol-rich foods lowers the amount left in the blood, and this helps prevent heart attacks.)

Foods especially high in this potentially dangerous substance include egg yolks and organs such as the liver, kidney and brains. Saturated fats such as lard and chicken fat, and fatty dairy products such as cream cheese and hard cheese, butter, cream or milk are also high in cholesterol. While none of these foods needs to be eliminated from all but the strictest of diets, they should certainly be eaten less frequently. Unsaturated fats, on the other hand (also called monosaturated fats), either lower – or have no effect on – blood cholesterol levels, depending on how unsaturated they are. Olive and peanut oils, for instance, neither raise nor lower cholesterol levels. But polyunsaturated fats such as corn, sunflower, soybean, safflower, walnut and sesame oils actually lower the amount of cholesterol circulating in the blood. So, we should eat less fat generally, but as we do need some in our diet, we should therefore favour the unsaturated or polyunsaturated oils. But, be warned, it takes twice as much polyunsaturated oil to lower the cholesterol level as it takes saturated fat to raise it.

Since individual susceptibility varies, obviously not everyone on a 'Western' diet dies of a heart attack, stroke or cancer. People are resilient in some respects, vulnerable in others. But nearly two-thirds of the population will succumb to one of these fatal illnesses and even if we don't suffer any ill effects from too much fat, salt and sugar, somebody we know, feed, or care for, will.

Most sadly, our eating habits are affecting our children. Fed on junk food – sausages, hamburgers, chips, cakes, etc. – they are learning dietary habits that will continue into adult life. Artery clogging starts in childhood and advances rapidly during one's twenties. By building up so much cholesterol, many young people are heading for a heart attack by the time they reach their forties, or they will have developed other health problems which may well lead to premature death. The safest, and simplest, thing to do would be to cut down on fat from childhood.

Fortunately, coronary heart disease develops very slowly, so changing our diet can have a very positive effect. With less cholesterol in the blood, there will be less damage to the arteries, and studies of people who change their eating habits show that their risk of disease changes correspondingly. A recent poll in the United States stated that two-thirds of the population had changed their eating habits for health reasons, while in the last 15 years, death from heart disease in the United States and Australia has decreased by 25 per cent. So positive action can produce positive results.

It's all very well to recommend eating less fat and cholesterol but far better to show you how, so here are some guidelines:

Trim red meat well and limit the portions to 125–175 g/4–6 oz, preferably eaten no more than once a day.

Choose chicken, turkey and other poultry in preference to red meat, discarding the skin, and any visible pockets of fat, before cooking.

Eat all the fish you want, so long as it is not fried or packed in oil.

Skim off the fat from stews, stocks and casseroles. This is easier if you cool them first, skim, then reheat to serve.

Limit egg yolks to no more than four per person per week, though use all the egg whites you want as they are fat-free.

Use a non-stick pan with little, or no, vegetable oil to cook meat and poultry. Or grill it, or put it in the home-smoker (page 15) for delicious and unusual flavours. Fish can also be home-smoked or cooked in their own juices in foil with little or no fat. Most of my recipes have no more than 15 g/½ oz (1 tablespoon) fat per serving, and cooking with such small amounts of fat, I use the finest ones of all: the best unsalted butter, olive oil, walnut oil and sunflower oil.

Avoid fried foods, but if you occasionally indulge, use a vegetable oil, preferably a polyunsaturated one, for frying, then drain the food well on absorbent paper.

Switch to skimmed, or lower fat, dairy products such as skimmed instead of whole milk, plain yoghurt instead of soured cream, and Ricotta or other curd cheeses instead of cream cheese. Use a small amount of strongly flavoured cheese such as Parmesan instead of a larger amount of a milder cheese, such as Cheddar. Cut down generally on hard cheeses as most of them are 30–40 per cent fat by weight.

Use less butter or margarine (preferably a soft polyunsaturated one) at the table or none at all. Good wholemeal bread, for instance, doesn't need it. On potatoes, be they jacket, boiled or steamed, use plain yoghurt, skimmed milk cheese or lots of chopped fresh herbs with lemon juice.

Eat fewer cakes, pies and biscuits and bake them yourself using polyunsaturated margarine and egg whites instead of whole eggs. Better still, bake fat-free sponges and sweetened yeast breads as low-fat substitutes for cakes.

Eat more dried peas and beans as a main source of protein.

Eat less peanut and other nut butters, fewer avocados and nuts. Though free of cholesterol, and low in saturated fat, they ARE fattening.

Avoid or limit processed snack foods; like most fast foods, they contain large amounts of fat, salt and sugar.

Especially lethal are the processed sugars such as commercial jam and the processed sugar and fat confections. These are a concentrated form of food energy, thus very dense in calories. Such highly processed foods keep for long periods since they contain not only chemical additives to 'improve' the flavour and texture, but also high levels of solid (saturated) fats, salt and sugar, replacing the moisture content which makes food spoil quickly. (Think how rapidly a damp potato goes rotten – crisps keep for ever!) More concentrated, thus easier to package and display on shelves, highly processed foods are (un)naturally less fibrous than natural foodstuffs which have more food value. Fresh fruits and vegetables, for instance, are bulky and seasonal; they bruise easily and go bad. Their freshness makes them good food but a bad marketing commodity.

As we in the West are so keen on highly processed foods, it isn't surprising that another conclusion of the NACNE report is that we eat too much salt and sugar, seven-tenths of the salt and two-thirds of the sugar being hidden in processed foods. The resulting problems are often related to the circulatory and digestive disorders caused by fat. For instance, too much salt can cause high blood pressure (hypertension) and strokes (brain haemorrhage), while excess sugar rots your teeth and can lead to diabetes, so it's wise to cut the amount of salt and sugar in your diet, as well as fat.

Adding salt to any of the recipes in this book is of course up to you but it seems to me that in most dishes salt obscures the ingredients' natural flavour, while lemon, or lime, juice and fresh herbs often bring it out. Try using less salt gradually and you'll see. If the people you cook for like salt, let them add it at the table, but use a coarse-grained salt such as rock or flake sea salt. They will inevitably use less because the pieces are larger than granular salt.

Particularly as people age do their systems become less able to tolerate fat. Vague complaints such as general lethargy, mild stomach upsets or headaches may be fat-related and eating less fat will often lessen or banish the symptoms completely. There can be other unexpected benefits. One of my relatives insisted that my low-fat cooking helped her arthritis. She avoided red meat and red wine, while citrus juice was another no-no, but all in all she definitely wasn't as stiff. Since then I've learned that, certainly for severe cases, a diet low in fat is important for arthritics.

Changing one's eating habits happens gradually, even if you live alone and cook for yourself. Cooking for a family can be more difficult; time is usually short and likes and dislikes are pretty definite. But you could ease them into lighter eating with the recipes in this book. Try a recipe similar to one you already cook, and serve it, with family favourites, as part of a meal. You'll probably find that the new dish is as delicious, light and stylish as the one you usually cook – and that your family is not against sampling more low-fat cuisine.

And even if you don't want to eat low-fat food all the time, interspersing a few low-fat dishes, or a few days' low fat cooking, into the normal routine will give you an enjoyable contrast between styles of food, and heighten your taste for more hearty fare. Try it and see, maybe in hot weather, or when you've had a blow-out on rich foods over Christmas or on holiday. After a binge you (and your digestive system!) will really enjoy coming back to low-fat eating and will find that even a day of it can make you feel, and look, better. It's also a good way to diet on the quiet and dinner party guests – also sneakily dieting – may well say a silent thank you.

Buying fresh ingredients is also cheaper, and more inspiring, than buying packaged food. Many supermarkets have enormously increased the number of fresh items they sell, but it's still more fun having a leisurely chat with the butcher or greengrocer about what they recommend, even if you only have time to do it occasionally. It's also more exciting watching the seasonal changes – the first fresh herbs in the garden or market, the first locally grown asparagus or strawberries, the arrival of knobbly, delicious nutty Jerusalem artichokes, or the cheering sight of bright Seville oranges in the grimmest months of winter.

Alcohol, too, has its part to play in a low-fat diet, though if you, like me, have problems digesting fat, you may also suffer the unpleasant effects of too much alcohol sooner and longer than other merrymakers. *Small* amounts of alcohol, though, seem to change the way the body handles cholesterol and in the process may help prevent heart disease. Several major studies have shown that, on average, people who have one or two alcoholic drinks a day have fewer heart attacks and live longer than non-drinkers. Unfortunately, *more* than two drinks a day raises the risk of heart disease.

For a quick meal or snack when you're away from home, remember to choose items such as fresh vegetables, fruit, yoghurt or curd cheese whenever possible and forgo most commercial fast foods. Be wary, too, of hard cheeses, sausages, meat pies and pasties, mayonnaise or salad cream in salads, gâteaux and biscuits. Food from vegetarian establishments is fine as long as their interpretation of 'vegetarian' doesn't stretch to cream.

Low-fat eating in restaurants is tricky but possible. Traditional Anglo-Saxon fare glories in lamb, beef and butter with lashings of cream. Unless it's an occasional treat, skip over the red meat offerings and choose poultry, fish or seafood dishes. Safest bets when eating out are grilled, steamed or poached dishes, avoiding those served with cream or cheese sauces. If you are unsure of the restaurant's particular menu jargon, ask the staff for a translation. It's also sensible to avoid fried foods. Batters sometimes contain egg yolks but, worse, the frying fat used in many restaurants is a cheap blend containing palm and coconut oils, both super-high in saturated fats. If you must compromise for hunger or politeness-sake, eat the chicken or fish, but push as much of the batter as possible to the side of the plate.

For starters, reasonable choices are raw vegetables with vinaigrette sauce, melon, steamed mussels or clams, and clear soups, but avoid pâtés and terrines unless made of vegetables set in aspic. Decline mayonnaise-based sauces and mayonnaise-dressed creations; even if you know that the mayonnaise is made with an oil high in polyunsaturates, egg yolks will be in there, too. Vinaigrettes are possible as a light dressing, as are all vegetable accompaniments unless they are fried, but request them with lemon juice – and no butter.

Fruit salads, sorbets, water ices and jellies are acceptable desserts. Sadly, little else is. Baked sweets are usually filled with butter and eggs; mousses, ice creams and custards suffer from a surfeit of eggs and cream.

Ethnic restaurants often offer more scope. The beautiful raw fish dishes, *sushi* and *sashimi*, on Japanese menus get high marks as low-fat choices, as do the many soups and simmered (*nabe*) or grilled (*teriyaki*) fish and chicken dishes.

In Chinese restaurants, where the small amount of vegetable oil used in stir-frying is commendable, stick to chicken, fish and vegetable dishes. The eggs used to bind some of the satiny sauces, garnish certain soups and flavour some fried rice, I'm afraid puts those dishes on your 'B' list. *Dim sum* dishes of steamed poultry, fish and shellfish delicacies make better low-fat fare.

Unless you're eating Bengali, Indian restaurants traditionally offer little fish. Chicken is best eaten in establishments which offer tandoori-baked foods otherwise it might have been cooked with *ghee* (clarified butter). Compensations are the delicious rice mixtures, *biryanis*, and the subtly flavoured pulse accompaniments, *dal*. When perusing the bread section of the menu, pass over the *parathas* – also made with ghee – and the *puris* which are puffy and light but fried in oil. Better bread choices are *chapatis*, *nan* and *tandoori roti* eaten with yoghurt instead of butter or ghee.

Be on guard in restaurants serving French fare, for the glories of its classic cuisine are butter, egg yolks and cream. Even *nouvelle cuisine* 'lightness' is dangerously misleading, as the *nouvelle* sauces are thickened not with flour but with reductions of cream and egg yolks. The advantage, though, of the *nouvelle* menu is that it usually has a much wider range of fish dishes with which we can 'console' ourselves. French restaurants of all persuasions generally have succulent goodies such as grilled or poached fish, seafood or poultry, and items steamed in foil *papillotes* or served with olive oil and tomato sauces. Dishes christened *à la provençal* or *à la marengo* indicate we low-fatties won't starve.

With all the pasta, eating *a l'italiano* offers more choice than French food, but avoid northern Italian specialities made with meat, cream, fatty cheeses and bacon, *pancetta*. Creamy avocados filled with prawns should be admired from a distance, but don't send back seafood salads unless yours is still swimming in olive oil. *Marinara* (tomato), *vongole* (clam) and *olio* (oil) sauces are best choices for pasta. If you feel at all cheated, have an extra spoonful of grated Parmesan.

Don't be despondent. The object of eating – out or at home – is to relax, and enjoy yourself. It's just a little more complicated in our busy world with all its prepackaged temptations. Most people don't have to follow a low-fat diet all the time. For those who want to or have to in order to avoid lethal complications, I've given a lot of detail, covering all the relevant points. If you only want an occasional day, week or month of delicious low-fat fare – or just want the information – consider this book a guide through the minefield of fat. Its recipes will show you how enjoyable low-fat eating can be. To stay on a 'diet', it must be pleasurable as well as beneficial. And I've stayed on mine for over ten years. As I said, sacrifice is not one of my strong points . . .

GLOSSARY

Aspic jelly powder is sold in airtight foil packages and is useful to have on hand. Making your own aspic and clarifying it with egg whites and shells can be great fun, but not when you've got a million other things to do plus five souls coming to dinner. Buy aspic powder at delicatessens and good food stores and to improve the flavour add a few drops of dry sherry or Madeira when mixing the powder with hot water.

Balsamic vinegar is a fine Italian condiment made of red wine and aged for several years. Mellow, with a hint of sweetness, its flavour is sublime on salads even without oil. Buy it at good delicatessens and speciality food stores.

Black mustard seeds (see mustard).

Blood oranges are a variety of orange with sweet reddish juice and a tight, thin skin that is fairly hard to peel. They usually appear in late winter for a brief season, so I buy them in quantity to squeeze and freeze the juice in ice-cube trays to keep on hand all year round. Blood oranges are the classic addition to make hollandaise sauce, low-fat or otherwise, into lovely, pale pink Maltoise sauce.

Borage flowers are small, deeply bright blue, edible – and the main reason for growing that decorative herb. The pretty flowers have no flavour, but the leaves are redolent of cucumber though very prickly and hairy – prized mainly by lovers of Pimms.

Bresaola is cured, dried beef fillet which has been matured for about two months to a deep red colour. It is expensive but delicious and is sold in fine slices, usually for an appetizer or special garnish.

Butter is a highly saturated fat which should be used in small amounts as an occasional treat, not as an everyday addition to bread, vegetables, sauces and soups. As a rare indulgence, it's worth buying the best unsalted, or lightly salted, varieties to enjoy butter's own special flavour. For this reason I have specified unsalted butter throughout the book, but if you prefer it, lightly salted butter makes a perfectly good substitute, particularly as the amounts used are small.

Cardamom is a sweet, highly fragrant spice, best bought as whole, small, cream-coloured, pale green or brown pods. Available in many supermarkets and oriental food stores, the pods are lightly crushed to release the small black seeds, which should be ground before using. Avoid buying ready-ground cardamom as it loses both fragrance and flavour, and it can be adulterated.

Cheese comes in many varieties and most are wonderful. Unfortunately, many of them are very high in saturated fat and so should be eaten only very occasionally. Cream cheeses are the worst offenders, followed closely by hard cheeses such as Stilton, Cheddar, Roquefort and Double Gloucester. Unless you actually like low-fat Cheddar or other cheese substitutes, it's better to use a small amount of the real thing to add flavour to a dish or, where you can, use an even smaller amount of grated Parmesan.

Parmesan, like Romano, is a hard, dry, strongly flavoured Italian cheese. Both are cheaper, and better, if bought in a piece from delicatessens, stored – wrapped loosely in muslin at room temperature – then grated a little at a time, as necessary.

Ricotta is a mild, fairly low-fat, unsalted Italian curd cheese which can be used more frequently than the harder cheeses on a low-fat diet. Delightful when it's fresh and moist, Ricotta is sold at many cheese counters and in Italian delicatessens. Store it, uncovered, in the refrigerator and use within two days of purchase.

Low-fat soft cheese, Quark, Fromage Blanc and other skimmed milk cheeses, are bland but can be used with impunity as they contain minuscule amounts of fat.

Chocolate is a mixture of cocoa, varying amounts of sugar and *lots* of saturated fat. Elevate it to occasional, special-treat status and use the finest varieties. Never, however, insult yourself, or your guests, by using chocolate cake covering which is artificial and horrid.

Consommé (canned) is useful to keep on hand when you have no homemade stock. Since it contains salt, canned consommé should not be used in dishes which are greatly reduced as they will become too salty.

Cornmeal, or ground maize, has a rich, almost nutty flavour. It comes in yellow and white varieties and is sold in many wholefood stores.

Dried mushrooms must be rehydrated before using, but they have a much stronger flavour than fresh ones; the soaking water is an added boon to use in cooking. Dried ceps – *cèpes* in French or *porcini* in Italian – are expensive delicatessen items, but a few go a long way. Chinese dried 'black' mushrooms – *shiitake* in Japanese – are sold in Chinese grocers and are also pricey, especially the better quality ones which paradoxically are pale brown and mottled in colour.

Eggs are good food but their yolks are high in cholesterol. Nutritionists reckon that we should eat only three to four a week, preferably not at the same meal. Egg whites, however, contain no fat, so they should be used wherever possible in place of whole eggs.

Freeze-dried green or pink peppercorns (see peppercorns).

Green garlic is the leaf of the garlic plant, which can be snipped periodically, like chives, to use in salads: simple to grow, and an interesting herb for the kitchen. Peel several cloves and plant them, fat-end down, in a sunny spot, covering them with soil and watering well. The leaf varies in pungency according to the variety used, so it's fun to plant several different types.

Margarine doesn't taste nearly so good as the best, unsalted butter and by law must contain the same amount of fat. Most margarines – even ones labelled 100 per cent vegetable oils – are highly saturated and should be avoided. If you want to use margarine for cooking or spreading, choose one labelled 'high in polyunsaturates'; if used instead of butter it will drastically reduce the amount of cholesterol in baked foods.

Marjoram flowers are violet coloured, with a very delicate flavour. Edible, they are pretty sprinkled into salads, or over grilled or smoked fish and poultry.

Milk, unless needed for young children or calves, should be skimmed. Skimmed milk contains less than 0.3 per cent cream (fat), tastes light and refreshing, and is sold fresh and pasteurized, or heat treated and sterilized (UHT). The latter is very useful to have on hand, in quantity, for cooking as it keeps for several months, unopened, without refrigeration.

Mustard is a low-fat condiment, excellent with many foods. It ranges in flavour from the smooth, mildly tangy Dijon mustards to the hot and sweet German ones. Whether smooth or grainy, our tastebuds can revel in mustards enhanced by whisky, herbs, peppercorns, olives, brandy, honey, champagne and even fruit. Heat destroys mustard's sharpness so, for a strong, mustard flavour, add it at the last minute to heated foods and sauces.

Mustard seeds (preferably black for decorative purposes) make lovely additions to many savoury dishes. Their flavour is nutty and they can be bought at most Asian grocers and good delicatessens.

Nuts are fatty, but most are also low in saturated fat and high in polyunsaturated fat. Shelled almonds, pine nuts (also called pine kernels), pistachios and walnuts are cheaper bought in quantity in wholefood stores, then stored in airtight containers in the freezer to keep them fresh.

Oils are fats which are liquid at room temperature, so they should be used sparingly on a low-fat diet. The best ones to choose are polyunsaturated named oils made from corn (maize), soya, sunflower or safflower, or unsaturated (monosaturated) oils such as peanut or olive oil.

Best for dribbling on salads are extra-virgin (cold-pressed) olive oils, walnut and hazelnut oils. The latter two need refrigeration and all are expensive, but beautifully flavoured. Fortunately only a little of their magic is required in any dish.

Pasta is cheap, filling and excellent for low-fat meals, unless it is served with a rich sauce. Dried pasta is convenient and comes in many shapes; fresh pasta can be made or bought, then stored, chilled, up to two days and cooks in much less time than the dried varieties.

Peppercorns (green) are the unripe berries of the plant *Piper nigrum*. Pungent rather than hot, they are canned or bottled in vinegar or brine, or are freeze-dried to remove all their moisture so they can be sold dried. Usually available from good delicatessens and speciality food stores.

Peppercorns (pink) aren't peppercorns at all, but the berries of the plant Schinus terebinthifolius. They are very pretty with a mild pungency and, like green peppercorns, are available steeped in vinegar or brine, or freeze-dried and sold at speciality food stores.

Pulses, the source of protein for many of the world's poor, the edible dried seeds of beans and peas, contain no fat and are high in complex carbohydrates, vitamins, minerals and in soluble fibre which helps to lower cholesterol in the blood, thus reducing the risk of heart disease. (Insoluble fibre such as that in wheat bran does not do this, though it does have other, digestive, benefits.) Pulses are also inexpensive and incredibly versatile.

Saffron is the stigma of the *Crocus sativa* flower and expensive, since it can only be gathered by hand. Always buy saffron strands (powdered saffron can be adulterated) and soak in warm water for 20–30 minutes to bring out the yellow colour and heavenly flavour.

Sage flowers are delicate, pale violet and absolutely delicious, having a milder flavour than the leaves. They make a pretty garnish to sprinkle over many vegetable, fish and poultry dishes.

Salt is essential for health, but we need it only in tiny quantities. There is usually enough salt in the vegetables and dairy foods we eat, but too much in the condiments. Excessive salt intake can cause high blood pressure (hypertension), and strokes, particularly if there is a family history of these diseases.

It's better to cook with little or no salt and let people add more, if necessary, at the table. Table salt is finely ground from rock salt and usually contains magnesium carbonate to keep it free flowing. Sea salt is purer and comes in flakes and coarse or fine crystals, though these aren't as fine as table salt. It tastes saltier than table salt, so not as much is needed.

Commercial salt substitutes are low in sodium, but high in potassium and, to my mind, taste revolting. Lemon juice, fresh herbs and herb vinegars are far more pleasant salt substitutes.

Szechwan (or Sichuan) peppercorns have a numbing effect rather than the hot spiciness of black peppercorns, as they come from a different plant, *Zanthoxylum piperitum.* Buy them in Chinese groceries.

Tofu, or bean curd, is a type of no-fat, high protein 'cheese' made from soya bean milk. It is available, fresh, from oriental grocers and many healthfood stores as firm cakes, which keep in the refrigerator up to five days provided they are submerged in water, the water being changed daily. Tofu is more widely available in its softer, so-called 'silken form', sold in sealed, aseptic (sterilized) cartons which can be kept, unopened, at room temperature for several weeks.

Vegetable bouillon (powdered) can be mixed instantly with water, is useful in lieu of homemade stock, and less salty than most stock cubes.

Vegetable stock (concentrated) is a paste which can be diluted with hot water to make a good flavoured stock. Useful when you have no homemade stock, it is also less salty than most stock cubes.

Yoghurt, plain, low-fat or Greek-style, allows low-fat foodies to enjoy many dishes once denied us because of their cream content. Low-fat yoghurt contains 0.5–2 per cent fat (very low-fat less than 0.5 per cent); while at the other end of the scale are Greek and Greek-style yoghurts with 9–10 per cent fat, ewe's milk (sheep's) yoghurt sitting in between with 6–7 per cent. Since double cream contains about 48 per cent fat, even the richer yoghurts are only one-fifth as fatty.

Greek and Greek-style yoghurts are thicker, with creamier textures than plain, low-fat yoghurts, but their flavours are similar – clean and slightly tart – though yoghurt made from ewe's milk tastes a little sharper. Substitute low-fat yoghurt for Greek or Greek-style (or ewe's milk) yoghurt or vice-versa, as your preferences will vary with the occasion, or dish you are cooking.

NOTES ON THE RECIPES

Use either metric or imperial measurements in any one recipe, not both, as the two systems are not exact equivalents.

The measurements used in this book are graded. The biggest spoon is 1 tablespoon or 15 millilitres, the second is 1 teaspoon or 5 millilitres, while the two smallest measure ½ and ¼ teaspoon, 2.5 and 1.5 millilitres respectively. All the spoon measurements are level unless stated otherwise.

Cooking times are approximate. There are so many variables – the size and type of food, individual oven and grill temperatures, heat conductivity of pans, etc. – that these times should be taken as general guidelines. Familiarity with your own cooking equipment is essential for the best results.

The suggested number of people a recipe will serve is also approximate, as this depends on individual appetites and what else is being served.

Many of the recipes do not specify quantities of salt, or do not mention salt at all. Increasing awareness of the health risks of eating too much salt has led to a general shift towards using less salt in our food. As many of the canned and bottled ingredients we use in cooking already contain substantial amounts of salt, dishes as a rule should be tasted for seasoning at the end of cooking and salt added only if necessary.

I have included recommendations for side dishes, garnishes or vegetable accompaniments in some cases but have not tried to present whole menus, which I leave to the reader.

HOME SMOKING

Home smokers are small, lightweight metal boxes, which add delicious possibilities – and variety – to low-fat eating, as no extra fat is needed to cook a range of succulent smoked foods. The smokers are as inexpensive, and easy to use, as small Hibachi barbecue grills but they are more compact and much less messy, since they are fired from underneath by little dishes of methylated spirits which never touch the food or sawdust.

The sawdust – which gives the beautiful, smoked flavour – is enclosed in its own, easy-to-clean compartment. Brooks make a size which will smoke eight whole trout but mine is their smaller version – easily accommodating four whole trout, fish steaks, chicken joints, or meat fillets.

Smokers should always be used outside, well away from open windows. You can then enjoy the appetizing smell, without the smoke, and without scorching your kitchen floor.

Poultry, or game of the feathered variety, fish of all kinds, as well as the more usually seen trout or salmon cutlets, can be successfully and easily smoked to give you a delicious treat – at under half the price that you would pay in the shops.

SOUPS

DUCK SOUP

TOMATO-CLOVE SOUP

Tomato-clove soup, jellied

CHILLED ORANGE AND LEMON SOUP

JACK'S DRUNKEN MUSHROOM SOUP

GAZPACHO

PERFECT LETTUCE SOUP

THICK ASPARAGUS SOUP

SORREL AND POTATO SOUP

Watercress and potato soup

LENTIL AND GAMMON SOUP

FENNEL AND BEETROOT SOUP

CARROT AND WATERCRESS SOUP

TURNIP AND POTATO SOUP

FLAGEOLET GARLIC SOUP

MEDITERRANEAN SHRIMP SOUP

ONION SOUP

PARSNIP, PEAR AND APPLE SOUP

YELLOW OR RED PEPPER-YOGHURT SOUP (*see Poultry*)

Soups are great crowd pleasers. The only fat in mine is a little oil, used initially to brown or sweat the vegetables. Or, maybe, the yoghurt stirred in just before serving, instead of cream. The satisfaction and quiet joy of making, and serving, soup almost equals the pleasure of eating it. While it simmers, soup lends a sense of stability to a kitchen and further rewards the cook when he or she ladles out its goodness.

Economy, and soup, are the main reasons I make stock from any kind of meat or poultry – be it bones, leftover joints and carcasses, or scraps bought for the purpose. For the sake of soup, I keep on hand the finest – i.e. lightly salted Swiss – vegetable bouillon granules and paste. And, though most are poor and oversalted, a few brands of canned consommé – not the most expensive by any means – can improve some soups, so I like to keep a few cans in the storecupboard.

My soups usually reflect the season's fresh vegetables and, often, its main courses too. For leftovers always find their way into the soup pot. Even if they can't be used immediately, small portions from a stew, casserole or vegetable dish are frozen until suitable partners can be found for them. And many a gastronomic delight has emerged from a marriage between two or three of those little containers.

DUCK SOUP

To Americans, Duck Soup is synonymous with the Marx Brothers – Europeans know better, however. Here is an audaciously good version, which will satisfy everyone's sense of a good time – and good eating!

Homemade duck stock takes time but otherwise is no trouble, so when you next serve duck (pages 119, 120) prolong the pleasure by preparing duck soup.

12–24 hours making the stock, then cooling and chilling, plus about 30 minutes

Serves 4
  1 duck carcass, plus wings
  2 bay leaves
  4 spring onions, green tops sliced into 25 mm/1 in lengths, bulbs cut into rings
  450 g/1 lb brussels sprouts, trimmed and, if large, cut in half lengthways
  700 g/1½ lb potatoes, cut into large dice
  1–2 teaspoons powdered vegetable bouillon, preferably Swiss
  about ½ small white cabbage, finely shredded
  ½ teaspoon caraway seeds, bruised in a pestle and mortar or with a rolling pin
  salt (optional) and freshly ground black pepper
  dill sprigs, to garnish

Remove and discard any fat from the duck carcass. Put it, with the wings and bay leaves, into a large saucepan. Cover with cold water and place the pan over the lowest heat possible. Even better is to use a heat-diffusing mat so the stock simmers really gently. When you are confident that the heat is constant (and will not go out, should it be gas) let the stock cook 12–24 hours – the longer the better.

When the stock is ready, reduce it by rapid boiling to about 575 ml/1 pint and strain through a sieve, reserving the bones. Let the stock cool, then chill it overnight; you can then easily skim off any remaining fat which will have risen to the top. Strip the meat off the bones, then discard them with any skin from the carcass and wings. Tear or chop the meat into small pieces, cover and chill.

When ready to make the soup, put the duck stock – which should be nicely jellied – into a large saucepan with the reserved meat. Add the onions, brussels sprouts and potatoes. Bring the mixture to the boil, then cook gently until the sprouts and potatoes are tender. Stir in the powdered vegetable bouillon, shredded cabbage and caraway seeds, and cook for another few minutes until the cabbage is tender but still slightly crisp. Season with salt, if wished, and pepper. Serve steaming hot, garnished with dill sprigs, accompanied by crusty bread and a fine salad.

TOMATO-CLOVE SOUP

Sterling Kinney, a Texan cook and friend, introduced me to this simple soup, scribbling the recipe over dinner. Its remarkable flavour has begun, and enlivened, many dinner parties for me. As it will for you.

about 1½ hours

Serves 6
  1½ tablespoons polyunsaturated oil
  1 small onion, coarsely chopped
  350 g/12 oz carrots, coarsely chopped
  2 celery sticks, chopped
  4–5 parsley sprigs
  1 litre/1¾ pints tomato juice
  1 bay leaf, crumbled
  20 cloves
  sprig of thyme or ½ teaspoon dried thyme
  ½ teaspoon freshly ground black pepper
  400 ml/14 fl oz canned beef consommé

For garnish
dill sprigs, or low-fat croûtons (page 175)

Heat the oil in a large saucepan over a medium-low heat. When hot, add the onion, carrots, celery and parsley, and cook for 5–6 minutes, stirring occasionally. Add the tomato juice, bay leaf, cloves, thyme and pepper. Bring to the boil, then reduce the heat, cover, and simmer gently for 1 hour.

Strain the liquid through a sieve, pressing on the vegetables to extract as much flavour as possible. Return the strained soup to the pan and stir in the consommé. Reheat gently, taste and add salt, if wished, then serve garnished with dill sprigs or low-fat croûtons.

- In warm weather it's a nice idea to gel the finished soup. Sprinkle 2½ tablespoons powdered gelatine over the hot soup, then stir it well in. Let the soup cool slightly, pour it into a large shallow container and chill overnight. To serve, cut into cubes and pile into bowls. Delicious topped with a little low-fat soured cream (page 42).

CHILLED ORANGE AND LEMON SOUP

Cold soups are a pleasure to make, because they are simple; a treasure to serve, because you can make them ahead; and a refreshing treat, for both cook and honoured guests.

45 minutes, plus cooling and chilling

Serves 6
   850 ml/1½ pints chicken stock (page 37)
   2 shallots or 1 small onion, chopped
   2 celery stalks, chopped
   3 medium-sized carrots, chopped
   5 parsley sprigs
   1 bay leaf, crumbled
   175 ml/6 fl oz freshly squeezed orange juice
   4 tablespoons freshly squeezed lemon juice
   4 medium-sized eggs
   2 medium-sized egg whites
   salt (optional) and freshly ground white pepper

For garnish
fresh coriander leaves or finely chopped parsley

Bring the chicken stock to the boil in a saucepan with the chopped vegetables, parsley sprigs and bay leaf, then simmer gently for 30 minutes. Strain the stock through a sieve, pressing on the vegetables to extract as much flavour as possible. Stir in the orange and lemon juices.

Beat the eggs and egg whites together in a small bowl, then whisk in about 150 ml/¼ pint of the strained stock. Pour the egg mixture into the rest of the soup, whisking continually. When cool, chill the stock until quite cold, 3–4 hours.

To serve, season with salt, if wished, and pepper, then sprinkle over a few coriander leaves or a little chopped parsley.

JACK'S DRUNKEN MUSHROOM SOUP

Highly recommended on many counts, not least because it is based on a recipe by the famous American cookery writer, Roy Andries de Groot, not my aunt who first claimed it. This is a soup to show off at all your best dinner parties, be they for two or twenty. It freezes beautifully, so I make it in triple quantities, storing it in small portions. Defrost slowly, then reheat it just before serving.

45 minutes

Serves 4–6
   450 g/1 lb button mushrooms, wiped with a damp cloth, stalks
      trimmed if necessary
   275 ml/½ pint dry white wine
   1.3 litres/2¼ pints skimmed milk
   40 g/1½ oz butter
   1 medium-sized onion, chopped
   1 medium-sized carrot, chopped
   1 celery stalk, chopped
   celery leaves or 2–3 lovage leaves, chopped (not essential, but they
      make a delicious addition)
   1 garlic clove, chopped
   25 g/1 oz parsley, chopped with stems
   4 tablespoons flour
   1 bay leaf, crumbled
   ½ teaspoon ground mace
   about 225 g/8 oz plain, Greek-style yoghurt

For garnish
finely chopped parsley (optional)

Slice the mushrooms and put them into a heavy saucepan with the white wine. Cover tightly and cook over a medium-low heat until the mushrooms are tender, about 10–15 minutes.

Meanwhile, heat the milk in a small saucepan until very hot, but not boiling. Remove from the heat. In another pan, melt the butter over a medium heat, then add the onion, carrot, celery stalk, and leaves if using, garlic and parsley. Cook, stirring frequently, until the onion begins to brown, then sprinkle in the flour. Stir for a minute, then remove the pan from the heat.

Strain the milk (it should still be hot), and add to the onion pan gradually, stirring continually until all is smoothly incorporated. Add the bay leaf and mace and return the pan to a moderately low heat for 10–15 minutes. The liquid should not boil or the soup will taste scorched – you are aiming for a gentle infusion of the vegetables and spices. Strain the milk through a sieve into a large bowl, pressing on the solids to extract all their flavour, then return the milk to the saucepan.

Drain the mushrooms, reserving the liquid. Purée the mushrooms in a food processor or blender, then add, with the wine, to the milk.

You can now either cool the soup and pour it into a container (or containers) to chill or freeze, or you can reheat it and correct the seasoning. When it is piping hot, but not boiling, quickly place a large dollop of yoghurt into individual bowls, then pour in the soup. Stir each portion slightly for a lovely streaky effect and sprinkle with chopped parsley, if wished. Serve immediately.

GAZPACHO

'To make the finest and easiest gazpacho in the world,' I replied when asked for the hundredth time why there is *always* an unopened container of tomato juice in my refrigerator. It's made in no time, impresses everyone and doesn't upset my diet: a perfect dish!

10 minutes

Serves 4
1½ tablespoons freshly squeezed lemon juice
350 g/12 oz plain, Greek-style yoghurt
about ½ teaspoon tarragon vinegar (optional)
1 litre/1¾ pints chilled tomato juice
about 20 cm/8 in cucumber
2–6 drops Tabasco sauce
3–4 thin spring onions
freshly ground black pepper

For garnish
dill sprigs (optional)

Mix the lemon juice into the yoghurt and stir in tarragon vinegar – or not – to taste. Transfer the yoghurt to a food processor or blender, then process it with the chilled tomato juice, in batches if necessary, and pour into a large bowl. Add Tabasco sauce to taste.

Slice the cucumber, then cut the slices into tiny dice. Chop the spring onions across into tiny rounds and add them, with the cucumber, to the soup. Season with freshly ground black pepper and serve garnished, if wished, with sprigs of fresh dill.

- I sometimes make the soup up to 2 hours in advance and keep it chilled in the refrigerator, adding any garnish just before serving.

PERFECT LETTUCE SOUP

This is another 'second-helping soup' that I make in large quantities and freeze. Light, delicious and lovely, it is simplicity by another name.

making the chicken stock, then 30 minutes

Serves 6

2 large round lettuces, thick stalks cut out, the leaves finely chopped
40 g/1½ oz butter
1 small onion, finely chopped
2 tablespoons flour
575 ml/1 pint chicken stock (page 37)
275 ml/½ pint skimmed milk
225 g/8 oz plain yoghurt, at room temperature, stirred
salt (optional) and freshly ground white pepper
freshly grated nutmeg

Bring a large saucepan of water to the boil, stir in the lettuce and simmer for 2–3 minutes. Drain the lettuce through a sieve, then purée it in a food processor or blender, in batches if necessary.

Melt the butter in a large saucepan over a low heat, add the onion and cook, stirring occasionally, until the onion softens. Do not let it burn.

Sprinkle over the flour and stir for 1 minute. Gradually add the chicken stock and milk, then bring to the boil, and simmer gently for about 5 minutes to remove the taste of raw flour. Stir in the lettuce purée.

Remove the pan from the heat. You can now either cool the soup and pour it into a container to chill or freeze, or you can finish it for serving.

Whisk the yoghurt into the soup and season with salt, if wished, and pepper. Grate over some nutmeg and serve.

THICK ASPARAGUS SOUP

This lovely thick asparagus soup will make your guests, family, and you, feel quite pampered. If you insist on gilding this lily, stir in some thick yoghurt.

1 hour

Serves 6
　900 g/2 lb fresh asparagus
　25 g/1 oz butter
　2 large shallots, chopped, or the white part of 2 small leeks,
　　chopped
　1 large potato, cut into small dice
　850 ml/1½ pints chicken stock (page 37)
　150 g/5 oz plain, Greek-style yoghurt (optional)
　salt (optional) and freshly ground white pepper

For garnish
fresh chives, snipped into 4 cm/1½ in long lengths

Trim away and discard any tough ends from the asparagus, then scrape away any small triangular scales below the tip. Cut the spears into 25 mm/1 in pieces.

Bring 850 ml/1½ pints water in a large saucepan to the boil, add the asparagus and cook until tender, 10–12 minutes. Drain the asparagus, and let it cool, reserving the cooking liquid.

Melt the butter in a saucepan over a low heat, add the shallots or leeks, cover and cook for 3–4 minutes or until they are softened. Add the diced potato and chicken stock, bring to the boil, then reduce the heat and simmer until the potato is tender, 15–20 minutes.

Purée the potato mixture with the asparagus in a food processor or blender, in batches if necessary. Return the mixture to the pan with the reserved asparagus liquid. Taste and add salt, if wished, and pepper, then reheat the soup over a medium-low heat but do not let it boil. Remove from the stove, stir in the yoghurt, if wished, and serve with a sprinkling of chives. Alternatively cool, cover and refrigerate the soup if you wish to serve it chilled.

- You can also use the yoghurt as a garnish, instead of the chives, by pouring a little into the centre of each serving bowl, then swirling with a teaspoon to prettily streak the soup.

- For a faster soup use 700 g/1½ lb canned drained asparagus instead of fresh, and add 575–700 ml/1–1¼ pints extra chicken or vegetable stock in place of the asparagus cooking liquid.

SORREL AND POTATO SOUP

One of the most gentle yet delightful pleasures of the year is to step outside and cut a few sorrel leaves from the garden. Then you make this marvellously comforting, simple soup. (If you haven't a garden, a pot or window box on the sill will do – sorrel is very obliging.)

20–25 minutes

Serves 4
   1 tablespoon butter
   about 50 g/2 oz sorrel leaves, including stems, roughly chopped
   3 medium-sized potatoes, scrubbed
   425 ml/¾ pint skimmed milk
   salt (optional) and freshly ground black pepper
   about 4 tablespoons plain, Greek-style yoghurt

Melt the butter in a saucepan over a very low heat, add the sorrel, cover and cook for about 5 minutes or until the leaves are soft, shaking the pan occasionally.

Meanwhile, cut the potatoes into small dice. Add them to the softened sorrel with the milk and 425 ml/¾ pint water. Raise the heat and simmer the mixture gently until the potatoes are just tender. Season with salt, if wished, and freshly ground black pepper.

Put a tablespoon or so of yoghurt into individual bowls, then pour over the soup. Serve at once.

- The rest of the year I make this delicious soup using a bunch of chopped watercress, tough stems discarded.
- Be old-fashioned and make this as a lovely gift for friends 'grounded' with flu. Omit the yoghurt, transport it in a thermos flask, then it simply needs a gentle reheating.

LENTIL AND GAMMON SOUP

For people who love simplicity and good soup, here is a recipe to make in large quantities. It freezes beautifully.

1 hour

Serves 6
450 g/1 lb red split lentils, picked over
1 small gammon knuckle
1 large carrot, chopped
2 celery stalks, chopped
1.1 litres/2 pints canned beef consommé
freshly ground black pepper

Wash the lentils in several changes of water, then put them in a very large saucepan with the gammon knuckle and the chopped vegetables. Cover with the consommé, bring to the boil, then simmer for 45 minutes or until the lentils are soft.
Remove the knuckle bone from the soup. Take the meat off the bone, chop or shred it finely and reserve.
Purée the soup in batches in a food processor or blender until smooth. Add pepper, you won't need salt as the knuckle will provide enough. Stir the meat into the soup and return to the saucepan, then reheat over a low heat, stirring continually to avoid scorching, and serve.

• Using consommé as well as the knuckle bone gives a beautifully rich stock but the consommé can be omitted if necessary. Or you can use less, and make up the required amount of liquid with water.

FENNEL AND BEETROOT SOUP

45 minutes

Serves 6
700 g/1½ lb bulb fennel, trimmed
225 g/8 oz cooked, peeled beetroot
1.1 litres/2 pints chicken stock (page 37)
150 g/5 oz low-fat soured cream (page 42)
salt (optional) and freshly ground black pepper

Chop the fennel and beetroot finely, then put in a large saucepan. Add the stock, bring to the boil and simmer for 20 minutes or until the fennel is tender.

Briefly process the mixture, in batches, in a food processor or blender to a slightly coarse consistency. Reheat the soup, stir in the soured cream and add seasoning to taste. Serve immediately.

- If you haven't enough chicken stock, you can make it up to the necessary amount of liquid by adding some water.

CARROT AND WATERCRESS SOUP

45 minutes

Serves 6
   25 g/1 oz unsalted butter
   800 g/1¾ lb carrots (peeled if they are old), grated
   1 large onion, finely chopped
   1½ tablespoons flour
   850 ml/1½ pints chicken stock (page 37)
   1 tablespoon polyunsaturated oil
   4 rashers lean bacon, rind and fat removed, then finely diced
   bunch of watercress, stems discarded
   150 g/5 oz plain, Greek-style yoghurt
   salt (optional) and freshly ground pepper

Melt the butter in a large saucepan over a very low heat and add the grated carrots and onion. Cover and leave to soften, shaking the pan occasionally, about 5 minutes. Sprinkle the flour over the carrots and stir it in. Add the stock gradually, bring to the boil, then simmer for 15 minutes or until the vegetables are very tender.

Meanwhile, heat the oil in a small frying pan over a low heat, add the diced bacon and fry gently, until crispy. Drain on absorbent paper and reserve.

Purée the carrot mixture, in batches, in a food processor or blender. Return the soup, with three-quarters of the watercress leaves, to the saucepan and season to taste. Reheat gently, then remove from the heat, and stir in the yoghurt. Serve with the bacon and the remaining watercress leaves sprinkled on top.

TURNIP AND POTATO SOUP

50–60 minutes

Serves 6
    700 g/1½ lb small turnips
    225 g/8 oz potatoes
    25 g/1 oz unsalted butter
    850 ml/1½ pints chicken stock (page 37)
    150 ml/¼ pint skimmed milk
    150 g/5 oz plain, Greek-style yoghurt
    salt (optional) and freshly ground black pepper

For garnish
chopped parsley

Peel and chop the turnips and potatoes into small dice. Melt the butter in a large saucepan over a very low heat. Add the vegetables and cook for 10 minutes, stirring frequently to prevent burning.

Meanwhile, heat the stock in another pan. Pour it over the vegetables, bring to the boil, then simmer for 20 minutes, or until the vegetables are tender. Purée the soup briefly, in batches, in a food processor or blender. The texture should be slightly coarse.

Return the soup to the saucepan, stir in the milk then season to taste. When hot but not boiling, remove from the heat and stir in the yoghurt. Serve, sprinkled with chopped parsley.

FLAGEOLET GARLIC SOUP

These pale green, small, kidney-shaped beans, so loved by the French, make a chic though substantial soup. Just right for a cosy supper by the fire with friends, or *en famille*.

Overnight soaking, then about 5 hours cooking the beans, plus 15 minutes

Serves 4–6
    450 g/1 lb dried flageolet beans, soaked overnight
    2–3 celery stalks, chopped
    1 medium-sized onion, chopped

1 bay leaf, crumbled
1–2 tablespoons Vecon or other concentrated vegetable stock
salt (optional)

For serving
15 g/½ oz unsalted butter per person, softened
½ garlic clove per person, crushed
1 teaspoon finely chopped parsley per person
low-fat croûtons (page 175)

Drain and rinse the soaked beans, put them in a large saucepan and cover with plenty of fresh water. Bring to the boil, then simmer for about 1 hour. Drain and rinse again. Return the beans to the pan, cover with plenty of hot fresh water, then add the vegetables, bay leaf and vegetable stock paste and bring to the boil. Simmer for 3–4 hours until the beans are tender, adding more boiling water as necessary. The beans should be barely covered with stock when they are done.

Discard the bay leaf and coarsely purée the celery and onion with half the beans in a food processor, or in batches in a blender. Return the purée to the saucepan with the rest of the beans. Add some water to thin the soup, if wished, and taste, adding salt if necessary. Stocks of any kind – and people's palates – vary.

Mix together the butter, garlic and parsley and set it aside. When ready to eat, warm the soup over a medium heat, stirring continually, as thick soups tend to burn and, while carbon may aid digestion, it does not enhance the soup's flavour – or your reputation as a cook. Pour the hot soup into bowls, add some of the garlic butter, sprinkle with croûtons and serve.

• Make in large quantities and freeze this soup, by all means, but add the garlic butter and, of course, the croûtons when serving.

MEDITERRANEAN SHRIMP SOUP

Friends will think that you have trapped the essence of the Mediterranean in this soup, with its flavours of aubergine, tomatoes and wine – no matter that you made it in only 30 minutes.

30 minutes

Serves 6
  4 tablespoons olive oil
  2 medium-sized onions, sliced
  1–2 garlic cloves, chopped
  1 medium-sized aubergine, peeled, sliced 3 mm/⅛ in thick, then
    chopped
  700 g/1½ lb canned tomatoes
  225 ml/8 fl oz dry white wine
  4 teaspoons dried oregano
  200 g/7 oz canned shrimps, drained and rinsed
  2 tablespoons chopped parsley
  salt (optional) and freshly ground black pepper
  125 g/4 oz grated Parmesan cheese

Heat 3 tablespoons of the oil in a large saucepan over a very low heat,
add the onions and garlic, cover and let them sweat for 5 minutes. Add
the aubergine with the rest of the oil and cook, stirring occasionally,
until the aubergine begins to soften, about 5 minutes, then stir in the
tomatoes with their juice, the wine and oregano. Cook over a medium-
low heat until the aubergines are tender and the soup has reduced
slightly, 10–15 minutes.
  Add the shrimps, parsley, salt, if wished, and pepper, then, just
before serving, stir in the cheese.

  • Though this soup freezes well, don't add the garlic until you reheat it
    (chop and lightly fry it first – in a drop of oil), then add the Parmesan just
    before serving.

ONION SOUP

My favourite onion soup is deep golden brown, with a pure, almost
magical taste of onions. Its lovely colour comes not from meat stock but
from the onion skins, and slow cooking.

4–5 hours

Makes about 1.4 litres/2½ pints
  4–5 large onions
  15 g/½ oz butter
  salt (optional) and freshly ground black pepper

freshly grated nutmeg
freshly grated Parmesan cheese

Slice off the ends, peel, slice and divide the onions into thin rings, the thinner the better. When an onion becomes too difficult to slice into rings, lay it flat and slice it thinly. Tie the onion skins in a muslin bag and reserve them.

Melt the butter in a large, heavy-based saucepan over a very low heat, add the onions and season with a little salt, if wished, and pepper. Grate over plenty of nutmeg, cover and let the onions sweat until they are very soft, about 2 hours, stirring very occasionally.

Add the reserved onion skins to the pan and 1.4 litres/2½ pints hot water, bring to the boil, then simmer, partially covered, for 2–3 hours. Remove the bag of onion skins. To serve, grate 25–50 g/1–2 oz Parmesan into individual bowls, then pour over the hot soup.

- Make this in double quantities whenever you can. The cooking time remains the same – the extra can be frozen for another day.

PARSNIP, PEAR AND APPLE SOUP

When the season turns chilly and the leaves fall, don't despair – celebrate with this soup.

1 hour

Serves 6–8
3 tablespoons polyunsaturated oil
1 small onion, chopped
2 teaspoons ground coriander
450 g/1 lb potatoes, finely diced
700 g/1½ lb parsnips, cut into large dice
450 g/1 lb pears, peeled, quartered, cored and chopped
225 g/8 oz apples, peeled, quartered, cored and chopped
1.1 litres/2 pints chicken stock (page 37)
175–225 g/6–8 oz plain, Greek-style yoghurt, preferably at room
    temperature, stirred well
salt and freshly ground white pepper (optional)

Heat the oil in a large saucepan over a medium low heat, add the onion and sprinkle over the ground coriander. Cook for 2–3 minutes, stirring occasionally and reducing the heat if necessary to prevent the onion burning. Add the potatoes, parsnips, pears and apples to the pan, then stir in the stock. Bring to the boil, reduce the heat and simmer for 30 minutes or until the potatoes are soft.

Purée the mixture, in batches, in a food processor or blender and return to the pan. When ready to serve, reheat the soup, then take off the stove and stir in the yoghurt. Taste, add salt and pepper, if wished, and serve at once.

SAUCES, STOCKS, DRESSINGS AND RELISHES

CHICKEN STOCK
GAME STOCK
ESPAGNOLE SAUCE
Clarified butter
REMOULADE SAUCE, LOW-FAT STYLE
CHILLI JAM
LOW-FAT SOURED CREAM
LOW-FAT MAYONNAISE
TOFU MAYONNAISE
YOGHURT
TARRAGON VINEGAR
BASIC VINAIGRETTE
Pear vinaigrette
TOMATO VINAIGRETTE
Smoked chicken salad
RED AND YELLOW PEPPER SAUCES (*see Poultry*)
GREEN PEPPER-SHERRY SAUCE (*see Poultry*)
TROTTER STOCK (*see Poultry*)
HERB VINAIGRETTE (*see Poultry*)
TONNATO SAUCE (*see Poultry*)
BIGARADE SAUCE (*see Poultry*)
POMEGRANATE-WALNUT SAUCE (*see Poultry*)
MADEIRA SAUCE (*see Meat*)
LOW-FAT HOLLANDAISE SAUCE (*see Eggs*)
SPINACH-RICOTTA SAUCE (*see Eggs*)
SPICY RED SAUCE FOR DIPPING PRAWNS (*see Fish*)
LOW-FAT TARTAR SAUCE (*see Fish*)
ROQUEFORT DRESSING (*see Fish*)
'WET WALNUT' SAUCE (*see Fish*)
Blanched almond or cashew sauce
1000 ISLAND DRESSING (*see Salads*)
SWEET PICKLED GHERKINS (*see Poultry*)
TOMATO SAUCE (*see Pasta*)
GIARDINARA SAUCE (*see Pasta*)
BASIL OR MIXED SAVOURY HERB PURÉE (*see Pasta*)

Popularity and satisfaction as a cook — low-fat or otherwise — increases with a judicious use of stocks, sauces, dressing and relishes to enhance, but never overpower, one's cooking. My favourite, and most successful, recipes are included in this section, and throughout the book with the recipes they most frequently accompany. As a base, or added flavour, for other dishes, many of them can be prepared ahead and kept for one, two or more days. This helps enormously when assembling a quick but delicious meal, or a dinner party dish, at the last minute. It also gives you time to try them out with your favourite foods, and create your own culinary sensations.

CHICKEN STOCK

Fine chicken stock improves many simple recipes and is essential in low-fat diets, where flavour can be sacrificed along with fat and calories. Stock is easy to make and keep, thanks to freezers. It is also economical – both in terms of money and time. Ten minutes of your active attention is all that the stock requires; during the three or so hours it is cooking you can enjoy other pursuits.

10 minutes, plus 3 hours simmering

Makes 1.1 litres/2 pints stock
   1.4–1.8 kg/3–4 lb chicken
   1 medium-sized onion, unpeeled
   1½ teaspoons coriander seeds
   ½–1 teaspoon black peppercorns
   ½ teaspoon fennel seeds
   2 bay leaves, crumbled

Remove the skin from the breasts and discard it, then remove the breasts (page 101). Cut away the thigh-leg joints from the carcass and cut the thighs from the legs. Freeze the breasts and thighs, if wished, by wrapping each piece in cling film, then overwrapping in a freezer bag or foil; otherwise refrigerate and use them within 1 day.

Remove any pockets of fat and skin from the meat, then put the carcass (broken in half if necessary to make it fit more easily) into a large pan, about 2.8 litres/5 pints in capacity. Add the legs, thighs if using, and wings or wingtips with the onion – unpeeled to give the stock colour – and the rest of the ingredients. Fill the pan with cold water.

Place the pan over a very low heat. The slower the stock comes to a simmer – and the longer it cooks – the better the flavour will be. When the liquid becomes cloudy, after 45 minutes–1 hour, raise the heat slightly so the stock simmers gently and leave it to cook for another 2 hours or so.

Transfer the meat, carcass and onion to a plate to cool (see below). Strain the stock through a sieve to remove the rest of the ingredients and return it to the saucepan. Reduce the stock, by boiling it over a high heat, to about 1.1 litres/2 pints, or, if your storage space, like mine, is limited, to about 575 ml/1 pint or even less. Pour the delicious stock into a bowl and cool, before refrigerating some hours or overnight.

When you skim off the fat you will see that the stock is nicely jellied and delicious to eat with a spoon. Pour it into containers and freeze, or cover and refrigerate it for up to 2 days, ready to use in soups, sauces and pilavs.

- The flavours in the above stock are nicely balanced and suitable for most uses, but you can vary them by adding more or less, or different, herbs and spices. Do not, however, add salt to a stock. It should be added only, if necessary, to the dish the stock is going to improve.
- From one chicken bought for stock, there are the breasts and perhaps the thighs to remove for grilling (pages 99–101) and, once the rest of the meat has been simmered for stock, it can be stripped from the bones for salads (pp. 108–10), crêpes, or enjoyed on its own with remoulade and other spicy sauces. The simmered onion is also delicious.

GAME STOCK

You can make a wonderful stock by slowly simmering the carcasses of game birds, their giblets and any unused pieces of meat with a bay leaf, a few juniper berries, a bouquet garni and, perhaps, an onion, until the stock tastes strongly – about 2–3 hours. Strain the stock, then reduce it, if wished, by rapid boiling. Cool, chill and skim off the fat before storing to use in soups, stews and sauces instead of, or even with, chicken stock.

ESPAGNOLE SAUCE

Last-minute, impromptu, and yet the very finest cooking can be done almost leisurely when you have this sauce frozen and to hand, as it is the basis of so many other classic sauces and dishes. It takes two days to make espagnole sauce, also known as demi-glace, but during most of this time you need do nothing. And at the end of the second day, your sauce is as fine as those in many of the finest French restaurants.

About 5 hours on day 1, plus cooling, then about 3 hours, plus cooling

Makes about 850 ml/1½ pints or 30 frozen cubes of sauce
  4 tablespoons polyunsaturated oil, plus extra for greasing
  1.1 kg/2½ lb knuckle or shin of veal, cut into 5 cm/2 in dice
  1.1 kg/2½ lb knuckle or shin of beef, cut into 5 cm/2 in dice

3 large onions, sliced
350 g/12 oz carrots, sliced
2 celery stalks, sliced
1 pig's trotter, split lengthways
2 garlic cloves, crushed
25–50 g/1–2 oz fresh parsley
4 sprigs fresh, or 1 teaspoon dried, thyme
3 large bay leaves
8 black peppercorns, crushed
50 ml/2 fl oz clarified butter (see below)
50 g/2 oz flour
225 g/8 oz canned tomatoes, drained and chopped

Heat the oven to 240°C/475°F/gas 9. Meanwhile, lightly grease a large roasting pan with a little oil, then spread the diced veal and beef over the pan in one layer. Sprinkle over 2 tablespoons of the oil and cook and colour the meat in the oven for 45 minutes, turning it occasionally.

Stir 2 of the onions, 225 g/8 oz of the carrots and the celery into the tin and continue cooking for 15 minutes.

Transfer the meat and vegetables to a preserving pan or large soup kettle and add 4 litres/7 pints water. Rinse out the roasting pan with 575 ml/1 pint water and add this to the rest of the liquid. Add the split trotter, garlic, parsley, half the thyme, 2 of the bay leaves and the peppercorns. Bring the liquid to the boil, then reduce the heat and simmer for 3 hours, skimming occasionally.

Meanwhile, make a dark brown roux to thicken and colour the sauce. Heat the clarified butter in a heavy frying pan over a medium heat. When hot, remove the pan from the heat and whisk in all the flour as quickly as possible, making a smooth paste. Return the pan to a medium heat and cook, stirring occasionally, until the roux turns a rich chocolate brown, about 10 minutes. Towards the end of cooking, stir the roux more frequently and reduce the heat, if necessary, to prevent burning. Immediately remove the roux from the pan, cool and reserve it in the refrigerator.

When the stock has simmered sufficiently, remove the trotter and put aside to later strip off the meat for another dish. Strain the stock through a fine-meshed strainer and cool, uncovered. Remove the beef and veal from the strainer and save (see below). You will have about 1.7 litres/3 pints liquid. Refrigerate the cooled stock and later remove the solidified fat. Keep the stock chilled and use it within three days or freeze it, and the roux.

When ready to finish making the sauce, pour all but 275 ml/10 fl oz of the stock into a large saucepan over a medium-high heat and bring to simmering point.

Meanwhile, heat the remaining 2 tablespoons oil in a heavy-based frying pan over a medium-low heat and cook the rest of the sliced carrot and onion until the latter is transparent.

Put the roux in another saucepan and pour over about 575 ml/1 pint of the almost simmering stock, whisking until the roux is dissolved, then pour into the large pan of simmering stock, whisking until thoroughly blended. Bring to the boil, then simmer slowly, uncovered, adding the softened carrots and onions, together with the remaining thyme and bay leaf. Cook for 30 minutes, skimming frequently.

Strain the mixture through a fine-meshed strainer, pressing on the vegetables to extract their juices. Wash the pan.

Return the thickened stock to the pan and add the 275 ml/10 fl oz unthickened, fat-free stock. Bring to the boil and simmer for 30 minutes, skimming frequently. Stir in the tomatoes and simmer for another hour, skimming.

Strain the sauce through a chinois or fine sieve lined with muslin into a large bowl. Let the sauce cool completely before refrigerating or freezing. To freeze the sauce as cubes, pour it, while still liquid, into ice cube trays, then cool before freezing. Normal-sized ice cubes will give about 2 tablespoons or 25 ml/1 fl oz liquid. Once the cubes are frozen, transfer them to freezer bags or a covered container and keep them frozen until ready to use.

- To make clarified butter, melt 15–25 g/½–1 oz more butter than is needed for a specific recipe, in a small saucepan over a low heat. Skim off any foam which rises to the surface. Carefully pour off the pale clarified butter, leaving the whitish sediment, that settles at the bottom, behind. Clarified butter is important in this recipe (and many others) for its flavour, and also because it can be heated to a higher temperature than ordinary butter without burning.
- The simmered knuckle or shin and trotter meat will become deliciously rich and almost sticky. Enjoy it with pilav (page 162) and salad, with a pepper sauce (page 99), chilli jam, or other spicy accompaniments.

REMOULADE SAUCE, LOW-FAT STYLE

Rather than despair of never again eating spicy remoulade sauce in its rich mayonnaise base, Jack devised an even tastier low-fat version that is a food addict's – and hostess's – dream. Serve it to add piquancy to shellfish, fish, poultry and meats.

10–15 minutes

Makes 275 ml/½ pint sauce
    225 g/8 oz round lettuce, cored and finely sliced
    25 g/1 oz parsley sprigs, stems discarded
    4–6 large garlic cloves
    75 g/3 oz shallots, roughly chopped
    small handful of celery leaves, chopped
    75 g/3 oz Moutarde de Meaux or similar coarse-grained mustard
    2 tablespoons olive oil
    2–3 tablespoons freshly squeezed lemon juice
    1 teaspoon paprika
    about 3 drops Tabasco sauce
    salt (optional)

Purée the lettuce, parsley, garlic, shallots and celery leaves in a food processor, or in batches in a blender, pressing down the purée occasionally with a rubber spatula. Drain the purée through a sieve, and discard the liquid.

Return the drained purée to the food processor or blender, add the remaining ingredients and blend. Taste and adjust the seasonings, adding salt if wished. Serve at room temperature, or cover and refrigerate to serve chilled. Keeps refrigerated for up to 2 days.

CHILLI JAM

My secret weapon in the war against insipid food on a low-fat diet is this startling sweet and chilli-hot condiment. Add it to any meat dish or stir a spoonful, or two, into soups or sauces (page 130). And, if you're of my persuasion, serve it as an appetizer on a slice of crispbread with Ricotta cheese, a warning, and a wink.

20 minutes

Makes 850 ml/1½ pints jam
75 g/3 oz fresh chillies
275 g/10 oz green or red pepper, to match the colour of the chillies
1.5 kg/3¼ lb sugar
350 ml/12 fl oz cider vinegar
225 ml/8 fl oz bottle Certo (liquid pectin)

Chillies, like passion, can easily overcome, so be sure your kitchen is well ventilated when you make this jam. And wash your hands immediately after handling the chillies.

Slice off, and discard, the tough stem end of the chillies, then chop them finely. Do likewise with the green pepper. Put chillies and pepper into a very large saucepan with the sugar and vinegar and bring to a full rolling boil, stirring occasionally with a long-handled wooden spoon.

Timing carefully once a hard boil is reached, boil for 9 minutes and remove from the heat. (If the jam overcooks, it will begin to caramelize and the flavour, and sparkling appearance, will change.)

Stir in the Certo right away and pour the jam into sterilized, glass preserving jars and seal as directed.

- For less culinary clout, and notoriety, reduce or omit the seeds in the chillies before chopping them.
- My dearest friends so love this jam that I give it as a thank-you, birthday, Christmas, you-name-it gift. Now it's my gift to you.

LOW-FAT SOURED CREAM

What culinary joy and relief to discover that, like Roquefort dressing (page 95), a light but very delicious low-fat soured cream can be made with plain yoghurt. Better to be low-fat and lovely, than high-risk and fat.

1 minute, plus overnight chilling

Makes 150 g/5 oz
2 teaspoons soured cream
150 g/5 oz plain yoghurt

Stir the soured cream into the yoghurt, cover and refrigerate for 8 hours or overnight. If the yoghurt is pasteurised, or homemade and fresh, the low-fat soured cream will keep refrigerated for up to 4 days.

- Made with thick, plain Greek-style yoghurt, low-fat soured cream is richer and thicker and may be more to your liking, though it may go off sooner, in about 3 days.

LOW-FAT MAYONNAISE

Beautiful mayonnaise is a dream, but it can be a nightmare to digest and Lord knows it's fattening. Low-fat mayonnaise is far easier to make and digest, and no more fattening than plain thick yoghurt – which is what it is. Flavour it with chopped chives, spring onions or other herbs; with tomato purée, horseradish sauce or curry powder; with garlic, mustard or capers – all the seasonings, in fact, that can be added to oil-rich mayonnaise. *Bon appetit et bonne santé.*

2 minutes

Makes 225 g/8 oz
225 g/8 oz plain, Greek-style yoghurt
about 2 tablespoons freshly squeezed lemon juice

Stir the yoghurt and lemon juice together. Store, covered, in the refrigerator for up to 3–4 days.

TOFU MAYONNAISE

Tofu mayonnaise has a faintly nutty flavour which you may well prefer to the flavour of yoghurt mayonnaise, and it is undeniably delicious with certain foods like Jerusalem artichoke salad (page 59). Make it and see.

About 10 minutes

Makes about 225 g/8 oz
275 g/10 oz silken tofu or 225 g/8 oz firm tofu
2–2½ tablespoons lemon juice
2 tablespoons polyunsaturated oil
½–¾ teaspoon tarragon vinegar
⅛ teaspoon salt (optional)
pinch of freshly ground white pepper

If using silken tofu, put it into the centre of a doubled, dry tea cloth and twist the ends together tightly. Press and knead the tofu gently in the cloth whilst holding the ends together tightly, for about 2 minutes, to expel some of the water.

Put the squeezed silken tofu (now about 225 g/8 oz), or firm tofu into a food processor or blender. Add the rest of the ingredients and purée for 15–20 seconds or until smooth.

Taste the mixture, adjust the seasonings, purée again briefly and serve or refrigerate, covered, for up to 2 days.

HOMEMADE YOGHURT

Cookery writer and friend Rosamond Man introduced me to the pleasures of making yoghurt and it's her we have to thank for this recipe. It's good to make before bed and enjoy warm and deliciously fresh for breakfast.

20–25 minutes, plus overnight standing, then 5–20 minutes

Makes 1 litre/1¾ pints
   1.1 litres/2 pints milk
   2 tablespoons live (unpasteurised) yoghurt

Heat the milk in a saucepan over a medium heat and, watching constantly, let it just come to the boil. When the liquid is starting to move towards the centre of the pan, immediately remove it from the heat.

Let the milk cool about 15–20 minutes, stirring occasionally, until you can barely hold your little finger in it for a count of 1001, 1002 . . . 1015. If you can comfortably hold your finger in for longer, briefly reheat the milk and let it cool until you can count to the magic 1015. If this seems too primitive for you, buy a yoghurt thermometer and let the milk cool to 41–43°C/106–109°F.

Spoon the yoghurt into a 1 litre/1¾ pint thermos flask and pour in the milk gradually, stirring briskly with a table knife. Screw the cap on the flask, leave it in a warm place and in about 8 hours the milk will have turned into yoghurt.

Put two bowls side by side with a sieve over one of them. Pour out some of the yoghurt into the sieve so the excess water drains off quickly, transfer the sieved yoghurt to the second bowl, replace the sieve and repeat until all the yoghurt is drained. The yoghurt-water is delightful, so drink it quickly before anyone else does.

For even thicker yoghurt, pour the yoghurt back into the sieve and let it drain into a bowl for 15–20 minutes. Transfer the yoghurt to a bowl, cover and refrigerate.

TARRAGON VINEGAR

Sharply fragrant and strongly flavoured with fresh tarragon, I use this, my favourite vinegar, every day, often on its own as a sprinkling for salads and vegetables, or to flavour other dishes. Save pretty bottles and fill them with this splendid vinegar to decorate the shelves of your kitchen; the vinegar can only improve with age.

5 minutes

Makes 1 litre/1¾ pints vinegar
  4–6 long branches of fresh tarragon
  1 litre/1¾ pints bought tarragon vinegar

Put 2 branches of the tarragon into each of 2–3 tall, slim bottles, cleaned and dried, and fill them with the bought tarragon vinegar. Make sure that the vinegar covers the tops of the branches, then cork or seal the bottles.

Display the bottles, but don't use them for at least a month when the flavour of the fresh tarragon will have become apparent. I now keep my tarragon vinegar a year before using it – unless I forget and give it all away.

- To make other herb vinegars, bring 1 litre/1¾ pints white wine vinegar to the boil, add fresh herbs, such as chervil, dill, sage or marjoram, cover, remove the pan from the heat and leave for 2 hours. Pour the vinegar into bottles, add a fresh sprig of the herb (discard the others), cork tightly and leave a month before using. Once opened, these vinegars tend to lose their lovely herby quality, so store them in small bottles. If you cannot buy tarragon vinegar, you can make it with this method, but, sadly, it won't last so long as the above recipe.

BASIC VINAIGRETTE

Well-made vinaigrette is a lovely dressing for salads; it's also a fine sauce with many variations and uses. So, it should always be well balanced: not too sharp from the vinegar and lemon, too piquant from the mustard and other seasonings, or too bland or unctuous from the oil. The oil itself should be polyunsaturated and mild, although walnut, hazelnut, sesame and olive oils are lovely for special vinaigrettes because of their distinctive flavours. My everyday choice is sunflower or safflower oil, though corn and soya oils are also good.

The technique of making a good vinaigrette is simple but brings many rewards, not least of which is regularly being asked to make the salad dressing at friends' dinner parties. Once you determine the proportion of ingredients that suits you, make it for any number, allowing 2 tablespoons (25 ml/1 fl oz) per person. Any leftover will happily keep, covered, in the refrigerator until the next day.

5–10 minutes

Makes about 225 ml/8 fl oz
    2 tablespoons finely chopped onion
    1 tiny garlic clove, crushed or finely chopped
    1½ tablespoons Dijon mustard
    pinch of salt
    a very little freshly ground white pepper
    2 tablespoons tarragon vinegar
    175 ml/6 fl oz polyunsaturated oil
    1 drop of Worcestershire sauce
    a few drops of freshly squeezed lemon juice

Mix the onion, garlic, mustard, salt, pepper and vinegar together with a hand whisk, then whisk in the oil. Taste and add a drop of Worcestershire sauce. If too much falls in, spoon out the extra. Whisk and taste again. Add the lemon juice, whisk and taste. You may decide that the sauce needs more of one, or some, of the ingredients, including oil, to balance the others, but always make tiny additions and taste after each one.

Changing any of the ingredients will have a great effect on your sauce. Variations on basic vinaigrette that I enjoy include the following: adding a few drops of red wine vinegar; doubling the amount of mustard to make a very thick, rich vinaigrette; using a flavoured smooth mustard such as green peppercorn, herb or black olive mustard with, or instead of, plain Dijon; using 2–3 garlic cloves.

- For pear vinaigrette, halve a pear and scoop out the seeds with a melon baller or teaspoon. Strain the vinaigrette into the centre of the pear halves.
- For boiled artichokes or raw vegetable crudités, basic vinaigrette is the perfect accompaniment.

TOMATO VINAIGRETTE

Tomato vinaigrette is one of those sauces whose flavour adds immeasurable elegance to a salad (see below).

5–10 minutes

Makes 150 ml/¹/₄ pint
    125 g/4 oz tomatoes, halved, seeded and chopped
    75 ml/3 fl oz chicken stock (page 37)
    1 tablespoon tomato purée
    2 tablespoons red wine vinegar
    2 tablespoons olive oil
    salt (optional) and freshly ground white pepper
    a few drops of lemon juice
    sugar (optional)

Purée the tomatoes in a food processor or a blender, then strain them through a sieve and whisk the pulp into the stock briskly, with the tomato purée and vinegar. Whisk in the oil gradually, then salt, if wished, and pepper to taste. Add lemon juice to taste and a very little sugar, if wished.

- Smoked chicken salad with tomato vinaigrette is one of life's delights and oh, so easy. Buy smoked chicken or smoke your own boned chicken breasts, about 1 per person, in a home smoker (page 15) for about 10 minutes. Slice the meat and arrange it on plates with a mixture of lettuces torn into bite-sized pieces, such as the tender inner leaves of round, cos, or lamb's lettuce, or curly endive. Using two or more different lettuces is important not just for the variety of 'greens', but for the flavour they will give to the salad. Spoon over the tomato vinaigrette; the recipe above will dress 4 servings.

APPETIZERS AND SALADS

TOSSED MIXED SALAD

AUBERGINE CAVIAR

FENNEL-CAULIFLOWER SALAD

ASPARAGUS QUICHE IN LETTUCE 'CRUST'

STRAWBERRY-WALNUT SALAD

1000 ISLAND SALAD

GAMMON AND GOAT CHEESE SALAD

LOW-FAT COLESLAW

ORIENTAL COLESLAW

JERUSALEM ARTICHOKE SALAD

MUSHROOM TERRINE IN LETTUCE 'CRUST'

CUCUMBER, MINT AND YOGHURT SALAD

Cucumber, basil and soured cream salad

SESAME ASPARAGUS SALAD

BANANA, MUSHROOM AND CELERY SALAD

'Salad', would be my reply, if I had to choose a favourite type of food. I simply adore the stuff, eat it at most meals including breakfast, even salads that have lingered from the night before. Whether anyone shares my morning eccentricity I know not, but I do know that salads add elegance, interest and balance to meals which might otherwise lack them. The number of dishes, and leftovers, enhanced by salads endlessly surprises me.

Freshly made, tossed mixed salads delightfully reflect the seasons. During the aptly named 'salad days' of warmer weather, the ingredients' different colours indicate variations in flavour, if not always texture. In chillier times, the paucity of the season requires ingenuity to make colourful, appetizing mixtures. Then especially is the time to make coleslaws and potato salads to serve with game and meat, or feast on alone.

Avocados apart, the 'fattiest' element of a salad is usually its dressing: oil in vinaigrettes, or dripped from the cruet or bottle. Avocado, like mayonnaise made from polyunsaturated oil, is a rare treat on a low-fat diet, but a spoonful of beautifully-flavoured vinaigrette is a very acceptable way to spend part of one's daily ration of fat. Generally, though, I select garden greens and herbs, toss them quickly into a bowl and am eminently satisfied with a dribble of walnut oil, or lovely green olive oil, and a squeeze of lemon juice or sprinkling of herb or wine vinegar.

Salads can certainly be appetizers, as many of the most delicious appetizers are raw vegetables or cunningly flavoured vegetable purées. Light and palate-prickling, these are often my choice to start a meal, or to serve as nibbles to keep a party going.

TOSSED MIXED SALAD

Variation is the nicest thing about tossed mixed salads. As the seasons arrive, all that's freshest and best can be included in the salad bowl. With the myriad oils and vinegars now available, and the sauces and dressings that can be made, the possibilities for delicious mixed and green salads are endless. They can be simple or elaborate, part of a meal or the meal itself, and need never taste the same.

When buying or gathering salad ingredients, choose various lettuces, herbs, onions, shallots, spring onions, tomatoes and cucumbers, to give a wide variety of textures, shapes, colours and flavours to the salad. Create interest with 'unusual' additions, such as sliced strawberries, blanched courgette batons, broccoli florets or tiny sliced new potatoes. Sliced mushrooms, sprigs of dill or mint leaves, thin ribbons or matchsticks of colourful peppers, a little grated carrot, pretty blue borage flowers or a few nuts will also add sparkle to your salad.

Prepare salads up to two hours in advance, before the pressures of cooking, or guests, descend. They will keep their 'freshness' by putting the acidic ingredients such as tomatoes, onions and similar flavourings at the bottom of the salad bowl, covering them fairly well with a layer of thin cucumber slices. The various greens, and the remaining ingredients, will stay crisp on top provided the salad is not dressed and tossed until just before serving.

Important to remember is that the greens should be clean and dried when they go into the salad bowl. The water from still-wet greens dilutes the flavour of vinaigrettes and other dressings. Just as crucial for an excellent salad is to thinly slice all ingredients (other than lettuce greens). Tasting a hint of each texture and flavour with every mouthful is glorious – biting into a hunk of cucumber, or slab of tomato, is not so winning.

A simple salad follows to give you the general idea: your combinations will obviously reflect the seasons, and your own preferences.

5–10 minutes

Serves 4
   1–2 firm ripe tomatoes
   2–3 spring onions, sliced at an angle
   3–4 small red radishes, thinly sliced
   ½ teaspoon drained capers, chopped
   salt (optional) and freshly ground black pepper
   4–5 cm/1½–2 in cucumber

a good handful each of 2 or more types of leaves, such as round,
    Webb's, cos or lamb's lettuce, sorrel, chicory, Chinese leaves,
    curly endive, tender dandelion leaves, red-leaved radicchio,
    spinach or watercress
fresh herbs such as chives, green garlic, chervil, dill, tarragon or
    parsley sprigs, sage, mint or lemon balm leaves (optional)

Cut out and discard the core from the tomatoes, slice thinly then spread
them over the bottom of the salad bowl. Distribute the spring onions,
radish slices and capers over the tomatoes. Sprinkle with a little salt, if
wished, and grind on black pepper. Remember if you are using a
vinaigrette or other salad dressing, it may already contain salt.

Slice the cucumber very thinly and spread the slices over the other
ingredients. Tear the lettuces and leaves into bite-sized pieces and put
on top of the cucumber slices. If using herbs, discard the stems, tear the
leaves, if large, and add them to the bowl.

Just before serving, sprinkle over oil and lemon (or vinegar), a little
balsamic vinegar on its own, vinaigrette sauce or another dressing, then
toss the salad well. Serve on largish plates to show off the salad's 'good
looks' as you feast on the subtle interplay of its flavours and textures.

AUBERGINE CAVIAR

When you're poor in pennies but rich in aubergines, try this recipe and
serve it with crispbread at your most elegant parties.

20 minutes, plus chilling

Serves 8–10
    3 large aubergines
    4 medium-sized tomatoes
    2 medium-sized green peppers, stems and seeds discarded
    1 medium-sized onion, roughly chopped
    4 tablespoons olive oil
    salt (optional) and freshly ground black pepper

Heat the oven to 190°C/375°F/gas 5. When hot, place the aubergines
(whole) on a baking tray and put in the oven for about 15 minutes, or
until the skins lose their gloss. Take out and cool slightly.

Meanwhile, immerse the tomatoes in boiling water for 30 seconds, drain immediately and put them under cold running water to stop them cooking, then skin them.

Remove the stems from the aubergines, then chop coarsely. Chop the tomatoes and peppers, then put all the vegetables and the oil in a food processor or a blender and purée. Season with salt, if wished, and pepper, then chill before serving.

FENNEL-CAULIFLOWER SALAD

A harvest festival of a salad, this seems to me – just right for tastebuds grown jaded after a season of wonderful salads. Try it – any time of year – and you'll see.

5 minutes

Serves 2–4
   2 medium-sized firm, ripe tomatoes
   salt (optional) and freshly ground black pepper
   1 bulb fennel, trimmed and thinly sliced
   2 medium-sized cauliflower stems, cut into small florets
   1 small, red onion, thinly sliced into rings
   3–4 fresh coriander sprigs, stems discarded
   3–4 cos lettuce leaves, cut across, 20 mm/¾ in wide
   1½ tablespoons olive oil
   1–1½ tablespoons tarragon vinegar

For perfection's sake I like to nick out the little hard stem end of the tomatoes before I slice them thinly and arrange in the bottom of a salad bowl. Season with a little salt, if wished, and pepper. Spread the fennel, cauliflower florets and onion rings over the tomatoes, then top with the coriander leaves and lettuce. Just before serving, dribble over the oil and vinegar and toss well.

ASPARAGUS QUICHE IN LETTUCE 'CRUST'

This is a fun dish, pretty enough to serve at the smartest of lunches.

about 1 hour

Serves 6–8
  unsalted butter for greasing
  350 g/12 oz fresh asparagus or 225 g/8 oz canned asparagus tips,
    drained
  salt
  425 g/15 oz plain, Greek-style yoghurt
  2 large eggs
  4 large egg whites
  large pinch of freshly grated nutmeg
  5–6 large Webb's, or round, lettuce leaves

  For garnish
  dill sprigs

Generously grease a 24 cm/9½ in sandwich tin. Cut silicone baking paper to fit the tin by drawing round its bottom and cutting strips 25 mm/1 in wide to line the sides. Press the paper into the bottom and sides of the tin, overlapping the side strips as necessary. Grease the top of the paper and set the tin aside.

If using fresh asparagus, trim away and discard any tough ends, then cut the spears diagonally into 25 mm/1 in pieces. Bring a large saucepan of water to the boil.

Heat the oven to 180°C/350°F/gas 4. Salt the boiling water, add the thicker pieces of asparagus and boil for 2 minutes. Add the asparagus tips and cook for a further 3 minutes or until the pieces are just tender. Drain, refresh the asparagus under cold running water, then drain again and dry on absorbent paper.

Whisk together the yoghurt, eggs, egg whites and nutmeg and pour the mixture into the prepared tin. Add the asparagus to the tin, distributing evenly and pushing the pieces into the liquid. Place the sandwich tin in a roasting pan and put it halfway into the oven. Pour boiling water into the roasting pan to come ¾-way up the side of the sandwich tin, slide the roasting pan into the oven and bake for 20–25 minutes or until the quiche feels firm to the touch and is just beginning to brown lightly on top.

Remove the roasting pan from the oven and the quiche tin from the water, then set aside for 5 minutes.

Turn a large plate upside-down over the quiche, then hold the quiche tin against the plate and invert. Lift off the tin and peel away any pieces of paper. Cut out the thick stalks from the lettuce leaves and cover the quiche with the leaves, their thin, curly edges outermost, extending beyond the edge of the quiche and curling downwards. Hold a serving plate upside-down against the lettuce and once again, very carefully, turn the plates over. The quiche will be surrounded by its lettuce crust. Garnish with dill sprigs and serve warm – with long white gloves and a smile.

STRAWBERRY-WALNUT SALAD

The flavour of the tomatoes and strawberries with the walnut oil makes this salad sheer bliss.

15 minutes

Serves 4–6
   3 medium-sized firm, ripe tomatoes, thinly sliced
   3–4 spring onions, bulbs thinly sliced, green tops cut into 25 mm/1 in
      lengths
   4–6 radishes, thinly sliced
   125 g/4 oz firm ripe strawberries, hulled, then thinly sliced
   1½ teaspoons chopped, fresh tarragon, or ½ teaspoon dried
      tarragon
   salt and freshly ground black pepper
   about 7.5 cm/3 in cucumber, very thinly sliced
   2, or more, varieties of lettuce leaves, torn into bite-sized pieces
   1 tablespoon walnut oil

Put the tomatoes into a salad bowl, then distribute the spring onions, radish and strawberry slices over them. Sprinkle on the tarragon, season with salt and pepper, then cover with the thin cucumber slices.

Arrange the torn lettuce leaves on top of the cucumber. Just before serving, dribble over the walnut oil and toss the salad well.

THOUSAND ISLAND SALAD

Refreshing, enticing, *and* low-fat, this is the ideal start to a meal. The crunchiness of the lettuce and tang of the dressing guarantees people will ask for more.

1 ¼ hours soaking and chilling the lettuce, then 10–20 minutes

Serves 4–6
    1 Webb's or Iceberg lettuce, washed, drained and chilled (see below)

    For the one thousand island dressing
    225 g/8 oz plain, Greek-style yoghurt
    2 tablespoons stoned, finely chopped black olives
    1 tablespoon finely chopped, canned pimientos
    ½ medium-sized hard-boiled egg, finely chopped
    1 tablespoon tomato ketchup
    ⅛ teaspoon crushed garlic
    2 tablespoons lemon juice
    ⅛ teaspoon Dijon mustard
    ⅛–¼ teaspoon Tabasco sauce
    1–2 drops Worcestershire sauce
    ¼ teaspoon coarsely ground black pepper
    pinch of salt (optional)

Mix together the dressing ingredients in a small bowl. Taste and adjust the seasoning, if wished, then cover and refrigerate unless serving immediately.

Cut the chilled lettuce in half, then shred it into coarse ribbons. Arrange the lettuce on individual serving plates, top with the dressing and serve immediately.

- To clean Webb's or Iceberg lettuce easily, hold the head between your hands with the core downwards. Knock it smartly on a hard surface until the core is loose, then pull out the core. Soak the lettuce in cold water for 10–15 minutes, then leave it to drain very well, shaking the head occasionally, about 30 minutes. Store it in the vegetable drawer of your refrigerator for at least 30 minutes.

GAMMON AND GOAT CHEESE SALAD

For an elegant starter, which can easily become a whole meal if you let it, try this low-fat version of a delicious French salad.

10 minutes

Serves 4–6
 450 g/1 lb curly endive
 50–75 g/2–3 oz Crottin de Chavignol or other sharp-tasting
   semi-firm goat cheese
 4 tablespoons olive oil
 225 g/8 oz lean, boneless gammon in one piece, trimmed of any fat,
   then cut into bite-sized pieces
 4–6 spring onions, bulbs finely sliced, green tops cut into 25 mm/
   1 in strips
 3 tablespoons wine vinegar, preferably red
 low-fat croûtons (page 175), defrosted if frozen

Cut the curly endive and cheese into bite-sized pieces and put into a salad bowl.

Heat the oil in a small saucepan over a medium-low heat. Add the gammon and spring onions and cook for about 1 minute. Remove the pan from the heat, stir in the vinegar and pour the mixture over the curly endive. Add a generous number of low-fat croûtons, toss the salad well and serve immediately.

LOW-FAT COLESLAW

Coleslaw is one of those 'moreish' salads which I strictly have to ration, otherwise I would happily eat nothing else.

15 minutes

Serves 6–8
 1 small firm white cabbage, any damaged outer leaves removed
 2–3 medium-sized carrots, scrubbed
 1 small onion, finely chopped
 ½ teaspoon dried dill weed or 1–2 sprigs finely chopped fresh dill
   (optional)

225 g/8 oz low-fat mayonnaise (page 43), or low-fat soured cream
  (page 42)
freshly ground black pepper

Quarter the cabbage and remove the core. Shred or grate the cabbage
and carrots either by hand, or in a food processor using a coleslaw
attachment. Transfer the cabbage and carrots to a bowl and mix in the
chopped onion and dill weed thoroughly.

Stir in the low-fat mayonnaise or soured cream, with freshly ground
black pepper to taste, and transfer to a smaller bowl to serve or
refrigerate, covered, and eat within 2 days.

ORIENTAL COLESLAW

My friend Yan-Kit So gave me this recipe some years ago and it has
since appeared in her splendid *Classic Chinese Cookbook*. As all at my
table adore the spicy flavour of ginger and Szechuan peppercorns, and
the salad keeps well, I usually make extra quantities of this for
'any-time-of-day' nibbling but especially to serve with roast game and
poultry, or smoked chicken.

5 minutes, plus 2–3 hours salting the cabbage; then 20 minutes, plus
  2–3 hours maturing

Serves 8
  1 small firm white cabbage, any damaged outer leaves removed
  2 tablespoons salt (see below)
  15–20 mm/½–¾ in fresh root ginger
  5 tablespoons sugar
  3 small dried red chillies
  2 tablespoons polyunsaturated oil
  2 tablespoons sesame oil
  1 teaspoon Szechuan peppercorns
  5 tablespoons rice vinegar

Quarter the cabbage and remove the core. Shred the cabbage finely with
a knife and put it into a large bowl. Sprinkle over the salt and mix it
through the cabbage, then leave for 2–3 hours at room temperature.
This will draw out much of the water content, and bulk. Squeeze the

water – and most of the salt – out of the cabbage, a handful at a time, leaving it damp, and transfer to another bowl.

Slice away the thin peel from the ginger and cut the piece in half lengthways. Cut each half into long, fine matchstick shreds, you need about 1 tablespoon, and place them in a bunch in the centre, and on top, of the cabbage. Sprinkle the sugar over the cabbage, taking care to avoid the ginger. Seed the chillies, cut them into paper-thin slices and reserve.

Pour the two oils into a small saucepan over a medium heat. When you see the first wisp of smoke, add the chillies and Szechuan peppercorns, then remove the pan from the heat. Pour the chilli mixture first over the shredded ginger – it will sizzle, and have a wonderful flavour – then over the surrounding cabbage. Pour over the rice vinegar and mix the salad well. Leave to stand at room temperature for 2–3 hours before serving. Warn friends not to eat the peppercorns, unless they are spice lovers!

It is said that this coleslaw keeps very well, covered, in the refrigerator for up to 2 weeks. Mine is always gone in a few days . . .

- To reduce the salt, drain and rinse the cabbage after salting and standing, drain well again and squeeze out the excess water by handfuls before proceeding with the recipe.

JERUSALEM ARTICHOKE SALAD

The sweet, nutty taste of Jerusalem artichokes is in perfect tandem with the subtle, nutty flavour of tofu mayonnaise. They make a rare picnic indeed when served as a salad with smoked chicken and dry white wine.

40 minutes

Serves 4–6
700 g/1½ lb Jerusalem artichokes, preferably not too knobbly
125–175 g/4–6 oz tofu mayonnaise (page 43)
small bunch of chives or the green tops of spring onions, thinly
    shredded lengthways, then cut into batons about 5 cm/2 in long

Scrub and wash the Jerusalem artichokes, then put them in a saucepan. Cover with plenty of hot water and bring quickly to the boil. Reduce the heat and simmer briskly for about 15 minutes or until they are tender but not soft when pierced with a fork. Immediately drain off the

cooking liquid and run cold water over the artichokes until they are
cool. Drain, then pat them dry on absorbent paper.

While the artichokes are cooking, make the tofu mayonnaise, and
chill until needed.

Slice the artichokes across into 'rounds' about 15 mm/½ in thick.
Put them in a serving bowl with half the chives or spring onion batons,
then stir in the tofu mayonnaise. Scatter over the rest of the chives or
spring onion batons just before serving.

- The salad will happily keep for one day, but after that the artichoke will
  begin to discolour.

MUSHROOM TERRINE IN LETTUCE 'CRUST'

Relax. This pâté has no meat in it, nor fattening pastry around it, just
the rich flavour of mushrooms to please you and your guests, whether
they are of a vegetarian, slimming or carnivore persuasion.

2¼ hours

Serves 6–8
    8–12 large lettuce leaves, preferably cos
    700 g/1½ lb button mushrooms
    25 g/1 oz unsalted butter, plus extra for greasing
    50 g/2 oz spring onions, chopped
    2 garlic cloves, crushed
    4 tablespoons dry sherry
    2 tablespoons lemon juice
    ½ teaspoon freshly grated nutmeg
    salt (optional) and freshly ground black pepper
    3 tablespoons flour
    2 large eggs
    2 large egg whites
    350 g/12 oz plain, Greek-style yoghurt

Bring a large saucepan of water to the boil and have ready a large bowl of
cold water nearby. Drop a lettuce leaf into the water for a few seconds,
until it becomes limp, then immediately transfer it to the cold water
while you repeat the process with the rest of the leaves. Drain, then dry

on absorbent paper and cut out the thick part of the central vein or core of each leaf. Set the leaves aside.

Cut baking parchment to fit the sides, bottom and top of a 900 g/2 lb loaf tin. Grease the inside of the tin generously and press in the paper, reserving the top piece. Grease the parchment paper in the tin and line the tin with the lettuce leaves, keeping enough back to cover the top and overlapping them to cover any holes.

Heat the oven to 190°C/375°F/gas 5. Wipe the mushrooms and chop them finely. Melt the butter in a large frying pan with a lid over a medium-low heat. Add the onions and garlic and cook for 30 seconds, stirring once or twice, then stir in the mushrooms. Cover the pan, reduce the heat a little and cook 10 minutes, stirring occasionally. When the juices are released, add the sherry and lemon juice and increase the heat slightly. Stir frequently to help evaporate the excess liquid and cook until the mixture is thick. Stir in the nutmeg, salt, if wished, and pepper to taste, then mix in the flour. Cook over a medium-low heat for 2–3 minutes, stirring occasionally, then set the mixture aside for about 10 minutes to cool, again stirring occasionally.

Beat the eggs and egg whites lightly and stir them gradually but thoroughly into the mushrooms. Add the yoghurt slowly but mixing well, then pour the mixture into the loaf tin and cover the top with lettuce. Butter the top piece of baking parchment and put it, buttered-side down, on top of the leaves. Set the loaf tin in a roasting pan in the oven and pour in boiling water to come halfway up the loaf tin. Bake the terrine for 1 hour, then remove it from the roasting pan to cool. After 15 minutes, loosen the terrine by running the edge of a sharp knife around the edges of the tin. Turn the terrine out on a serving plate and serve warm or cold.

CUCUMBER, MINT AND YOGHURT SALAD

Cucumbers are a happy standby in place of crisps when serving dips and hors d'oeuvres. Allied with the elegance of soured cream and pungency of mint, cucumber's fresh, juicy, and crunchy qualities are sensational.

5–10 minutes

Serves 4
   ½–1 cucumber, thinly sliced
   4–5 mint sprigs, stems discarded

1 teaspoon aniseed, freshly bruised in a pestle and mortar
juice of 1–1½ lemons
150 g/5 oz plain, Greek-style yoghurt, stirred

Mix the cucumber and mint and put into a shallow serving dish, or on individual plates. Sprinkle on the aniseed and lemon juice, then spoon over the stirred yoghurt, forking it in here and there to give an attractive appearance.

- Cucumber, basil and soured cream salad is a delicious variation on the above theme. Halve a cucumber lengthways, then cut into 15 mm/½ in dice. Mix with 8 basil leaves, cut into ribbons, and 3–4 chopped spring onions, about 150 g/5 oz low-fat soured cream (page 42) and coarsely ground black pepper. This also makes a superb filling for toasted pitta bread sandwiches.

SESAME ASPARAGUS SALAD

Just as often as you look forward to fresh asparagus, look forward to this salad.

20–25 minutes

Serves 6
350 g/12 oz fresh asparagus
2 tablespoons sesame seeds
1–2 heads round lettuce
6–8 small radishes
175 g/6 oz tightly closed button mushrooms, wiped with a damp cloth
1 small red onion, halved, then cut into semi-circular slices

For the sesame-soy dressing
50 ml/2 fl oz red wine vinegar
1 tablespoon soy sauce
50 ml/2 fl oz chicken stock (page 37), warmed slightly until liquid
1½–2 teaspoons sugar
3 tablespoons polyunsaturated oil (*not* olive)
1 teaspoon sesame oil
2–3 teaspoons peeled and grated fresh ginger root

Trim the tough ends off the asparagus. Diagonally cut the spears into pieces about 4 cm/1½ in long. Divide them into thicker and thinner groups.

Bring a large saucepan of water to a rolling boil. Drop in the thicker pieces and after 20–30 seconds drop in the thinner pieces. Cook the asparagus for 1–1½ minutes or until just tender. Drain off the hot water then let the pan overflow with cold running water until the asparagus is quite cold. Drain and dry on absorbent paper.

Dry-fry the sesame seeds in a heavy frying pan, stirring occasionally, until they are lightly brown. Transfer them to a bowl or plate and set aside.

Tear the lettuce into bite-sized pieces, leaving the small leaves whole. Slice the radishes and mushrooms thinly and add them to a salad bowl with the lettuce. Divide the onion slices into small sections and add them to the salad.

Whisk the vinegar, soy sauce, stock and sugar together in a small bowl. Then gradually whisk in the oils until the mixture is emulsified. Mix in the ginger and toss the dressing, with the asparagus, into the salad.

Sprinkle over the sesame seeds and serve at once.

- Sesame-soy dressing is a nice surprise for most green salads, though tomatoes are not so well dressed in it.

BANANA, MUSHROOM AND CELERY SALAD

Curious combinations sometimes make good marriages. This is a happy one indeed, perfect with crusty bread rolls.

15 minutes, plus 15 minutes maturing

Serves 6
350 g/12 oz button mushrooms, with tightly closed caps
3 medium-sized bananas
4–5 celery stalks, large 'strings' and tough bottoms discarded
150 g/5 oz low-fat mayonnaise (page 43)

Wipe the mushrooms clean with a damp cloth, then slice finely. Cut the bananas and celery stalks into slices about 20 mm/¾ in thick.

Mix the mushrooms, bananas and celery into the low-fat mayonnaise, cover and let the salad mature at least 15 minutes before serving.

EGG DISHES

GREEN PEA SOUFFLÉ

SAVOURY SURPRISE SOUFFLÉ

LEEK SOUFFLÉ WITH LEEK SAUCE

ASPARAGUS OMELETTE HOLLANDAISE

Sorrel/spinach omelette hollandaise

SOFT-BOILED EGGS WITH SPINACH-RICOTTA SAUCE

SOUFFLÉ BOUILLABAISE

TUNA AND ONION OMELETTE

SPICED DAL SOUFFLÉ

Eggs are magic in the kitchen. They perform an amazing number of culinary feats, from making meringues, binding meat loaves and raising soufflés to thickening sauces, glazing pastry and forming emulsions, either with butter for hollandaise sauce, or oil for mayonnaise. But egg yolks – not the whites – are high in fat (about 30 per cent), and particularly high in cholesterol. This is why experts now recommend that we eat no more than four eggs a week – preferably no more than one in any day.

A good solution is to reduce the number of egg yolks we use in dishes, perhaps by using more egg whites to compensate. You will see examples of this throughout the book. When I do use whole eggs, I like to make them seem as special as they really are. Each recipe in this section uses only one egg yolk per serving, with the exception of Asparagus omelette hollandaise. Without the low-fat (yes, really!) hollandaise sauce, the recipe does use only one egg yolk per serving and with the sauce, the dish is, as Eve purred to Adam, 'a justifiable sin'.

GREEN PEA SOUFFLÉ

Freshly picked, shelled and cooked peas have a sublime flavour. Alas, their season is far too short and access to really fresh green peas too limited. This elegant starter or lunch dish cheats the season with fresh pea flavour in a rich green, airy-light soufflé.

about 1¾ hours

Serves 6
   3–4 large lettuce leaves
   450 g/1 lb frozen peas
   3 spring onions, chopped
   ½ teaspoon sugar
   salt and freshly ground black pepper
   275 ml/½ pint skimmed milk
   40 g/1½ oz unsalted butter
   3 tablespoons flour
   4 large egg yolks
   6 large egg whites

   For garnish
   6 thin slices *bresaola* or *Bünderfleish* (air-dried beef)
   tiny radishes

Wet the lettuce leaves, gently shake and use them to line a 575 ml/1 pint soufflé or similar heat-proof dish. Pour in the frozen peas, then stir in the spring onions, sugar and season with salt and pepper. Cover the top of the dish well with foil. Put the dish, on a heat diffusing mat, over the very lowest heat for 50–60 minutes.

Meanwhile, gently bring the milk almost to the boil, then remove from the heat. Melt the butter in a shallow saucepan over a low heat. Add the flour and stir with a wooden spoon for about 2 minutes, but do not allow the mixture to colour. Remove from the heat.

Add the hot milk gradually to the butter and flour mixture, stirring continually until all the milk has been smoothly incorporated. Place the pan over a low heat and stir the mixture constantly for about 5 minutes until well thickened. Remove from the heat and pour the sauce into a large bowl. Stir it occasionally to help it cool. Heat the oven to 190°C/375°F/gas 5.

When the peas are ready, remove them from the heat and purée them with the lettuce leaves and spring onions in a food processor or blender. Stir the purée into the sauce, then stir in the egg yolks well.

Whisk the egg whites until they hold firm but are not dry peaks. With a hand whisk, stir one-third of the egg whites into the pea mixture then fold in the rest lightly and quickly.

Pour the mixture into a 1.1 litre/2 pint soufflé dish and place it in the lower centre part of the oven for 25 minutes or until it is well risen and feels firm when lightly touched on top.

Have ready serving plates garnished with the slices of air-dried beef and small radishes. Spoon on the beautiful green soufflé and serve immediately.

- The method given above for cooking frozen peas is useful for serving them as a vegetable accompaniment whether pureed or whole.

SAVOURY SURPRISE SOUFFLÉ

'Magician', people will call you and, knowingly, you'll smile. Soufflés are simple to make; it's exquisite low-fat cooking that's the art.

about 45 minutes

Serves 4–6
40 g/1½ oz unsalted butter, plus extra for greasing
2 tablespoons freshly grated Parmesan cheese
275 ml/½ pint skimmed milk
3 tablespoons flour
3 large egg yolks
salt and freshly ground white pepper
5 large egg whites
175 g/6 oz fairly firm goat's cheese such as Buche Raffec, very thinly sliced
2 tablespoons dried thyme

Heat the oven to 180°C/350°F/gas 4. Liberally grease a 1.1 litre/2 pint soufflé dish with butter and dust it with half the Parmesan cheese. Warm the milk until hot but not boiling.

Melt the butter in a saucepan over a low heat and stir in the flour. Cook for 1–2 minutes, stirring occasionally. Remove the pan from the heat and gradually pour in the hot milk, stirring continually with a wire whisk until the sauce is smooth. Return the pan to a slightly raised heat, and continue whisking until the sauce thickens a little.

Pour the sauce into a large bowl and let it cool, about 3 minutes, whisking occasionally. Whisk in the egg yolks thoroughly, seasoning with salt and pepper.

In another large bowl, beat the egg whites with an electric whisk until firm but not dry. Gently but thoroughly stir one-third of the egg whites into the sauce with a wire whisk, then pour the rest of the whites onto the sauce. With a rubber spatula or metal spoon, fold the egg whites into the sauce rapidly and lightly, turning the bowl as you do so. Do not overfold or the egg whites will deflate.

Pour half the mixture into the prepared dish and scatter over the goat cheese. Sprinkle with half the thyme and pour over the rest of the soufflé mixture. Smooth the top with a rubber spatula or the back of a metal spoon. Sprinkle the rest of the Parmesan and thyme over the top.

Bake for 25 minutes or until the risen soufflé is firm to the touch. Serve immediately.

LEEK SOUFFLÉ WITH LEEK SAUCE

The intense colour and flavour of the sauce twinned with the delicacy of this leek soufflé is a remarkably good way to begin a meal. You can cook the leeks the day before and make the sauce and soufflé on the day.

1½ hours to cook the leeks, plus 40 minutes

Serves 6
    1.1 kg/2½ lb leeks
    850 ml/1½ pints skimmed milk
    ½ teaspoon ground mace
    freshly ground white pepper
    40 g/1½ oz unsalted butter
    3 tablespoons flour
    4 large egg yolks
    6 large egg whites
    salt (optional)

Heat the oven to 180°C/350°F/gas 4. Cut the leeks in half lengthways up to their white ends, then give them a quarter turn and cut them through again into four. Wash them well, rubbing away any dirt.

Shake the leeks dry, then chop them to fit into a small deep casserole or tin and pour in the milk. Add the mace and pepper, seal the casserole or tin tightly with foil and bake for 30 minutes. Remove the tin from the oven, stir the leeks thoroughly, cover and return to the oven for a further 30 minutes or until the leeks are very tender. Drain the leeks and reserve the milk and leeks separately.

Heat the butter in a shallow saucepan over a low heat. Add the flour and stir with a wooden spoon for 2 minutes, but do not allow the mixture to colour. Remove the pan from the heat. Raise the oven to 190°C/375°F/gas 5.

Add the reserved milk, rewarmed if necessary, to the butter and flour mixture, stirring continually until all the milk has been smoothly incorporated. Place the pan over a low heat and stir continually for about 5 minutes until the mixture is quite thick. Remove the pan from the heat and pour the sauce into a large bowl. Stir it occasionally to help it cool, then stir the egg yolks into the cooled sauce.

Meanwhile, whisk the egg whites until they hold firm, snowy, but not dry, peaks. With a hand whisk, stir one-third of the egg whites thoroughly into the sauce to lighten it, then fold in the rest lightly and quickly. Pour the mixture into a 1.1 litre/2 pint soufflé dish or 275 ml/½ pint individual soufflé dishes or ramekins, and place in the lower centre of the oven for 25 minutes or until the soufflé is well risen and feels firm when lightly touched on top.

While the soufflé cooks, purée the reserved leeks in a food processor or blender, in batches if necessary, then rub the purée through a sieve into a bowl. Discard the contents of the sieve.

When cooked, remove the soufflé from the oven and serve immediately with some of the strained purée poured over each serving.

ASPARAGUS OMELETTE HOLLANDAISE

For those of us who can't survive without hollandaise sauce, this is the recipe. The knack of serving fresh asparagus omelettes for six is to have the asparagus and low-fat sauce ready. The omelettes should then only take about 10 minutes.

45 minutes

Serves 6
700 g/1 ½ lb asparagus (about 3 large spears per serving)
salt
6 large eggs
butter for greasing

For the low-fat hollandaise sauce
50 g/2 oz unsalted butter, chilled
2 medium-sized egg yolks
75–125 g/3–4 oz plain yoghurt, at room temperature
freshly squeezed lemon juice
cayenne pepper
salt (optional)

For garnish
6 small round slices of red pepper

Trim any tough ends from the asparagus spears. Lightly pressing each spear against the work surface, scrape away the small triangular scales below the tip with a potato peeler, or a sharp knife held almost at a horizontal angle, the blade pointing *away* from you.

Bring a large frying pan of water to the boil, add salt, then put the asparagus in the water, propping the thinner, upper parts of the spears against the rim of the pan, the tips out of the water. Cook for 3–4 minutes depending on the thickness of the spears, then ease the rest of the spears and tips into the water. Cook for 2–4 minutes or until the asparagus is just tender. Drain away the water, refresh the asparagus in the pan under cold running water, and drain.

For the sauce, cut the chilled butter into small pieces. Put the egg yolks in the top of a double boiler and whisk them with a piece of the butter. Place the pan over, not in, barely bubbling water, adding more cold butter as soon as one piece is melted. If the sauce seems to be getting too hot, incorporating the butter and thickening too quickly, lift the pan from the double boiler and continue whisking in pieces of cold butter off the heat. When the butter isn't melting so quickly, replace the pan over the water.

When all the butter has been absorbed, remove the whole double boiler from the heat, and the top pan from the water. Stir in the yoghurt, 2–3 teaspoons lemon juice, cayenne pepper to taste and salt if you wish. Replace the pan over the water in the double boiler to keep warm, but don't return to the heat.

Whisk the eggs in a bowl with 6 tablespoons warm water. Heat a

20 cm/8 in seasoned omelette pan, or frying pan with a flat bottom, over a medium-low heat and add about ½ teaspoon butter. Brush the melted butter around the pan and add about 3 tablespoons of the egg mixture, tilting the pan to cover the bottom and adding a little more egg mixture to cover any holes. Cook for about 1½ minutes or until the top of the omelette is almost dry. Using a palette knife or a rubber spatula, loosen the edges of the omelette, then slide it onto a warmed serving plate. Melt more butter and fry the rest of the omelettes in the same way. Meanwhile bring a large frying pan of water to a gentle simmer.

Add the asparagus to the simmering water for 1 minute to heat it through, then drain well on absorbent paper and divide the spears between the centres of the omelettes. Fold one side, then the other, over the asparagus. Don't worry if the sides don't meet or if the omelette tears.

Spoon a ribbon of sauce over each omelette, camouflaging any torn areas and spooning any extra sauce around the omelettes. Garnish with small round slices of red pepper and serve right away.

- Extra fancy canned asparagus spears are just possible in this dish if they are drained, then patted dry on absorbent paper, but a beautiful fresh substitute would be a handful, per omelette, of either sorrel or spinach leaves. Wash the trimmed leaves and put them over low heat for 5 minutes or until they become limp. Cover, and set aside while you make the hollandaise, then drain before using.

SOFT-BOILED EGGS WITH SPINACH-RICOTTA SAUCE

So simple is this recipe, it's a treat for the cook! And a dream to eat. Serve it for brunch, lunch or supper.

15 minutes

Serves 6
  12 medium-sized eggs

  For the spinach-Ricotta sauce
  450 g/1 lb frozen spinach, defrosted
  25 g/1 oz unsalted butter
  skimmed milk
  freshly grated nutmeg

salt and freshly ground white pepper
225 g/8 oz fresh Ricotta cheese
25–50 g/1–2 oz Parmesan or Romano cheese, freshly grated

For serving
green salad (optional)

To make the spinach-Ricotta sauce, squeeze the water from the spinach and chop it finely if necessary. Melt the butter in a saucepan over a medium-low heat, add the spinach and just enough milk to cover. Cook, stirring occasionally, until the milk has almost disappeared. Add nutmeg, and season to taste.

Stir the fresh Ricotta into the spinach and mix well, then lightly stir in the grated cheese, remove from heat, cover and keep warm.

Meanwhile, carefully lower the eggs into a large pan of boiling water, simmer for 4½ minutes, then drain and put them under cold running water for a few seconds until just cool enough to handle. Carefully shell the eggs, then quickly divide the sauce between 6 warmed serving plates and place 2 eggs on each portion of sauce. Serve immediately with a green salad dressed with walnut oil, if wished.

- Reheat spinach-Ricotta sauce by stirring a little more milk into the sauce over a low heat.
- Toss the sauce through hot pasta for another treat!

SOUFFLÉ BOUILLABAISE

Ask your fishmonger for white fish scraps to use in this recipe, as the more varieties you have the better.

30 minutes for the stock, then about 45 minutes

Serves 4–6
175 g/6 oz boneless, skinned mixed white fish
125 g/4 oz prawns, boiled and peeled
40 g/1½ oz unsalted butter, plus extra for greasing
275 ml/½ pint skimmed milk
3 tablespoons flour
3 large egg yolks

¾ teaspoon dried powdered orange peel (available from specialist
    food stores), or ½ teaspoon freshly grated orange zest
pinch of saffron
salt (optional) and freshly ground white pepper
5 large egg whites

For the court-bouillon
1 tablespoon fennel seeds, crushed
sprig of thyme or ½ teaspoon dried thyme
½ teaspoon dried powdered orange peel, or grated zest of 1
    medium-sized orange
1 bay leaf, crumbled
3 garlic cloves, lightly crushed
1 medium-sized onion, chopped
½ teaspoon black peppercorns, crushed

Put the ingredients for the court-bouillon into a saucepan with 850
ml/1½ pints water. Bring to the boil, then simmer gently for 30
minutes. Meanwhile, put the fish and prawns together in a food
processor fitted with the metal blade, then process 5–10 seconds or until
the fish is finely chopped but not pasty.

Strain the hot bouillon into another saucepan and place over a very
low heat. The liquid should not even bubble. Vigorously stir the
chopped fish mixture into the bouillon with a wire whisk for 10 seconds
and immediately strain the mixture, reserving the fish. Cool and freeze
the stock for using again if you wish.

Heat the oven to 180°C/350°F/gas 4 and liberally grease a 1.1 litre/2
pint soufflé dish with butter. Heat the milk gently until hot but not
boiling. Melt the butter in a saucepan over a low heat and stir in the
flour. Cook for 1–2 minutes, stirring occasionally. Remove the pan
from the heat and gradually pour in the hot milk, stirring continually
with a wire whisk until the sauce is smooth. Return the pan to the stove,
raise the heat slightly and continue whisking until the sauce thickens a
little.

Pour the sauce into a large bowl and let it cool, about 3 minutes,
whisking occasionally. Whisk in the egg yolks thoroughly, then stir in
the fish, orange peel, and saffron. Season with salt, if wished, and
pepper.

In another large bowl, beat the egg whites with an electric whisk until
the whites are firm but not dry. Gently but thoroughly stir one-third of
the egg whites into the sauce with a wire whisk, then pour the rest of the
whites onto the sauce. With a rubber spatula or metal spoon, fold the

egg whites into the sauce rapidly and lightly, turning the bowl as you do so. Do not overfold or the egg whites will deflate.

Pour the mixture into the prepared dish and smooth the top with a rubber spatula or the back of a metal spoon. Bake for 25 minutes or until the risen soufflé is golden brown and firm to the touch. Serve immediately, giving each person some of the crusty brown exterior.

TUNA AND ONION OMELETTE

French omelettes that fold over their fillings are fine, but another version, which a Swiss chef showed me, is easier to make, stays warmer for longer and has a height which is especially attractive. It's an excellent standby when you want a substantial meal quickly – particularly as you can vary the amounts of ingredients to feed any number.

about 10 minutes

Serves 2
2 medium-sized eggs
3–4 medium-sized egg whites
15 g/½ oz unsalted butter
½ small red onion, halved lengthways, thinly sliced and divided into semi-circles
50 g/2 oz canned tuna, drained and flaked
1 tablespoon chopped parsley
salt (optional) and freshly ground black pepper

Whisk the eggs and egg whites with 1 tablespoon water and set them aside. Melt the butter in a small omelette or frying pan over a low heat and add the onion. Cook for about 1 minute, then add the flaked tuna fish and parsley. Cook for another 30 seconds or so, then pour in the eggs and raise the heat slightly.

When the bottom of the egg mixture solidifies on the surface of the pan, stir once or twice with a metal, or heat-proof rubber, spatula to allow the liquid egg to reach the pan's surface. When it solidifies, after another 30 seconds or so, stir again. Add salt, if wished, and pepper and repeat stirring and cooking until you can push the egg mixture towards one side of the pan. Let the omelette cook until the eggs are as solid as you like them, then serve.

- For moister, less solid omelettes, cook them more quickly on a medium-high heat and stir less frequently.
- Additions to stir into this omelette are almost limitless – mushrooms, beansprouts, chopped meat or poultry, Ricotta cheese, pimiento or seeded sliced tomato, chopped sorrel or chicory.

SPICED DAL SOUFFLÉ

The pulses here are cooked in a traditional Indian way, then transformed with a bit of Western magic into a sublimely-flavoured, wonderfully textured soufflé.

about 1¼ hours

Serves 6
    275 ml/½ pint hot skimmed milk
    40 g/1½ oz butter, plus extra for greasing
    3 tablespoons flour
    3 large egg yolks
    4 large egg whites
    1 tablespoon chives, about 5 cm/2 in long (optional)

For the spiced dal
    225 g/8 oz moong dal, picked over (see below)
    1 small onion, halved lengthways, then sliced
    2 cinnamon sticks, broken in pieces
    ¾ teaspoon salt
    ½ teaspoon sugar
    1 small fresh chilli, seeded (optional) and chopped
    freshly ground black pepper
    2 tablespoons polyunsaturated oil
    1 teaspoon cumin seeds

First make the spiced dal by putting the pulses in a saucepan and washing them in cold running water until the water is clear. Drain, and add fresh water to cover well. Bring to the boil and simmer rapidly, uncovered, for 15 minutes.

Drain the pulses through a sieve, rinsing them in hot water. Return to the saucepan with the sliced onion and cinnamon, and add hot water to cover by 15 mm/½ in. Bring the water to the boil, reduce the heat and simmer gently for 25–30 minutes. Drain off any excess liquid; the pulses should be a soft, thick, and fairly dry mixture. Discard the cinnamon sticks. Remove the pan from the heat and add the salt, sugar, chilli and a liberal amount of freshly ground black pepper.

Heat the oil in a frying pan over a medium-low heat and add the cumin seeds. As soon as the seeds begin to pop, stir in the cooked pulses and heat them, stirring frequently, for 3–4 minutes. Put the mixture to one side.

Heat the oven to 190°C/375°F/gas 5. Heat the milk in a small pan until just simmering. Melt the butter in another saucepan over a low heat and stir in the flour. Cook for 1–2 minutes, stirring occasionally, then remove the pan from the heat and gradually pour in the hot milk, stirring continually with a wire whisk until the sauce is smooth.

Raise the heat slightly and continue whisking until the sauce thickens a little, about 5 minutes, then remove from the heat. Mix the sauce into the pulses and stir in the egg yolks.

Beat the egg whites in a large bowl with an electric whisk until the whites are firm but not dry. Stir one-third of the whites gently but thoroughly into the pulse mixture with a wire whisk, then fold in the rest of the whites with a rubber spatula or metal spoon. Gently and quickly fold in the chives, if using.

Pour the soufflé mixture into a greased, 1.7 litre/3 pint soufflé dish or 6 × 275 ml/½ pint ramekins. When done, the top of the soufflé will begin to brown and will feel firm to the touch. Serve immediately.

- Moong dal are a lovely olivey-green pulse sold by all Asian grocers and at many supermarkets. Because these lentils have been hulled and split they do not need soaking before cooking.
- The spiced lentils make a fine accompaniment to grilled poultry or soft-boiled eggs. The latter makes a delicious, warming and satisfying meal, so I make extra spiced lentils to freeze for easy winter suppers.

FISH AND SHELLFISH

SKATE IN ASPIC
Skate in jellied fish stock

POACHED COD IN 'WET WALNUT' SAUCE

SMOKED TROUT WITH WHISKY STUFFING

PRAWNS EN PAPILLOTE
Prawns en papillote with Pernod
Prawns en papillote with coriander seeds and onion
Prawns en papillote with nine low-fat sauces

BAKED BLACK MUSHROOMS AND COD
Fumet (fish stock)

SMOKED MACKEREL WITH RUM AND LIME

HALIBUT POACHED IN VEGETABLE-HERB SAUCE

CREOLE PRAWNS
Creole monkfish
Creole red snapper

TUNA WITH FLAGEOLETS

HONEY MUSTARD SALMON EN PAPILLOTE

SCALLOP AND PRAWN MOUSSELINE

STEAMED COD WITH FRESH TOMATO SAUCE

POACHED MONKFISH WITH ROQUEFORT DRESSING

Provided they are not fried, or canned in oil, fish and shellfish have far less fat than meat and, moreover, that fat is not so harmful. To take the most dramatic comparison, lean beef and veal cuts may have up to 15 per cent fat, whereas white fish such as cod, haddock and whiting contain less than 1 per cent. Marginally 'fatter' are plaice, prawns and scallops with under 3½ per cent, while even those so-called 'oily' fish – mackerel and herring – are excellent choices for the low-fat menu. Despite an apparently higher fat content than our lean meats, their fat (16 and 18 per cent respectively) is in fact far less saturated than that in red meat – and 20 per cent is actually polyunsaturated.

Real dangers on a low-fat diet are the butter, and other fat-rich, sauces, which traditionally accompany the delicious denizens of the deep. We can, however, enjoy our fishy friends with a clear conscience by cooking them without, or with only a very little, fat and adorning them with an array of low-fat sauces and dressings.

SKATE IN ASPIC

Before understanding my difficulty in digesting fats, skate swimming in brown butter with capers, *raie au beurre noir*, was my favourite fish dish. Later, with butter on the banned list, I used to pine for those long strips of delicately flavoured white flesh with its distinctive gelatinous quality, so I began to look for lower-fat ways to enjoy skate. Poaching the fish, then chilling it in aspic made up from packaged jelly powder, was an easy, elegant and truly pretty solution. One that I've also used successfully with many other kinds of fish – even inexpensive tail bits. As you can make the dish the day before, it makes a wonderful dinner party starter.

45 minutes, plus cooling the court-bouillon and fish, then chilling

Serves 4
   700–900 g/1½–2 lb skate wings
   1 packet good aspic jelly powder that makes about 425 ml/¾ pint
      aspic jelly
   3–4 tablespoons dry white wine (optional)
   2 tablespoons chopped fresh lovage, tarragon or chervil leaves, or ½
      teaspoon dried tarragon

For the court-bouillon
3–4 parsley sprigs
½ teaspoon black peppercorns, crushed
¼ teaspoon fennel seeds, bruised
1 small onion, roughly chopped
1–2 bay leaves
150 ml/¼ pint dry white wine or 4 tablespoons freshly squeezed
   lemon juice (optional)

For serving
curly endive salad

First make the court-bouillon (the poaching liquid) by adding all the bouillon ingredients (including the wine or lemon juice if you wish to use the bouillon for making the aspic – see below) to a saucepan filled with 850 ml/1½ pints cold water. Bring the liquid to the boil, simmer for 20 minutes, then strain and cool.

   Heat the oven to 190°C/375°F/gas 5. Cut the skate wings into serving pieces and put them in a roasting pan or ovenproof dish. If they smell faintly of ammonia, don't worry – this is quite normal and will disappear during the cooking. Pour over the cooled poaching liquid, adding some cold water, if necessary, to cover the fish. Put the pan carefully in the oven and poach for about 20 minutes or until the flesh flakes easily when tested with a fork. Remove the fish from the liquid and let it cool.

Meanwhile, stir the aspic jelly powder or crystals into 425 ml/¾ pint boiling water, add the wine, if wished, and the herbs, then let them steep in the liquids as it cools.

Put the fish in a large shallow dish or 2 soup plates with a little space between each piece and pour over the cool aspic liquid. Chill overnight or until the aspic is firm. Serve the skate in aspic with a curly endive mixed salad.

- To make skate, or other poached fish, in jelly, if you haven't any aspic jelly crystals, strain the poaching liquid through a muslin-lined sieve. Sprinkle over, then whisk in, 1 tablespoon powdered gelatine, add the herbs and wine, if wished, and cool before pouring the jelly over the fish.
- Cold poached skate with remoulade sauce (page 41) also makes a terrific meal! Who cares about old brown butter?

POACHED COD IN 'WET WALNUT' SAUCE

In the autumn of every year, be on the lookout – or ask – for 'wet walnuts', those young specimens with thin shells that crack easily to reveal blond rather than brown nuts. Available for about 1 month, the shelled nuts are delicious in themselves, but their walnut flavour becomes quite remarkable when the thin blond skin is peeled off the ivory-white meat. I never begrudge the patience and little time it takes to prepare this seasonal delicacy – especially as family and friends, once initiated in their delightful taste, are easily dragooned into helping. For one of autumn's delicacies awaits.

The sauce given in the simple recipe below is good with other blanched, unsalted nuts such as cashews or almonds, but with the once-a-year pleasure of 'wet walnuts', it is *quite* special.

Shelling the nuts, making and cooling the court bouillon, then 30 minutes

Serves 4
    12–16 wet walnuts or 3 tablespoons other blanched, unsalted
       chopped nuts
    225 g/8 oz plain, Greek-style yoghurt
    about 1 tablespoon freshly squeezed lemon juice
    freshly ground white pepper
    1 litre/1¾ pints court bouillon (page 81)
    4 × 175–225 g/6–8 oz cod steaks or other fish steaks, skinned

For garnish
    ½ teaspoon finely chopped dill, parsley, tarragon or other fresh
       green herb, or ¼ teaspoon dried dill weed

For serving
    mixed salad, dressed with olive oil and lemon juice

If using wet walnuts, shell them by crushing 2 against each other in the palm of your hand, pick off the shell and remove the nut. Peel each one by scraping up some of the pale skin and pulling it off to reveal the white meat beneath. Long fingernails are a distinct asset, though not an essential, for this operation. Once peeled, chop the nuts.

Mix the yoghurt with the lemon juice and chopped nuts, then grind in pepper to taste and put the mixture aside, at room temperature, while you make, and cool, the court-bouillon.

Heat the oven to 180°C/375°F/gas 5. Put the fish steaks, in one layer, in a small roasting pan or ovenproof dish into which they fit snugly. Pour the cooled court-bouillon over the steaks, adding cold water, if necessary, to cover them well, then place them in the hot oven. Cod steaks should be tender, moist and flake easily in 20 minutes; firmer fish like halibut and salmon take about 25 minutes.

Transfer the steaks to a warmed serving dish or individual plates, spoon over some of the sauce and sprinkle with a very little of your chosen chopped fresh herb. Serve immediately with a mixed salad.

SMOKED TROUT WITH WHISKY STUFFING

Tastebuds brighten when smoked fish is mentioned, so it is an inspired solution, particularly when you feel disenchanted with everyday cooking, or have a dinner party looming. Home smoking boxes are inexpensive, wickedly easy to operate, and small, usually accommodating four trout-sized fish, or eight, if you have the slightly larger version (page 15). One recipe I've served very successfully on several occasions is this. The whisky stuffing, smoked with the trout, makes a memorable combination.

about 40 minutes, plus cooling

Serves 4
    4 × 350–450 g/¾–1 lb trout, cleaned
    small loaf of good wholemeal bread, preferably unsliced
    8–12 tablespoons bourbon or scotch

For garnish
sage or marjoram flowers, or green tops of spring onions

For serving
mixed salad (optional)

Select smaller trout for a starter, larger ones for a main course, and rinse them well in cold water, then pat dry with absorbent paper. Remove and discard the crust from the bread, then cut the loaf into batons to fit inside the fish. You need enough batons to fill the fish and still be able to close its 2 sides. Put the batons on a plate and sprinkle over the bourbon or scotch. Stuff the bread into the cavities of the trout, then press the sides together. You can leave them for about 30 minutes in a cool place, or, if necessary, a little longer in the refrigerator.

Out of doors, sprinkle hardwood sawdust over the prescribed area of the smoking box, place the cover and rack on top, then position the trout on the rack. Place the lid on the smoking box. Fill and light the small spirit burners and place the smoking box over them. Let the fish smoke for about 20 minutes, refilling the burners if necessary. Let the fish cool about 15 minutes in the smoker.

Bring the trout into the kitchen and place them on your work surface. Cut through the skin round the base of each head and tail, then insert a table knife between the thin edge of the meat and skin at the cavity. Carefully lift up and pull away the skin from each trout, turning them over gently as you pull, giving a pink smoked trout with its head and tail. After the first one you'll see how easy and quick this is to do.

Place the trout on serving dishes and, if you have them, scatter over pale purple sage flowers in early summer, or tiny violet-pink marjoram flowers in late summer. Otherwise, finely shred 1–2 spring onion green tops lengthwise, then cut them diagonally into longish, thin batons and scatter over the smoked fish. Serve the fish as a starter or with salad, if wished, as a main course.

PRAWNS EN PAPILLOTE

Serving prawns in their shells, from the foil wrappings in which they are baked, is sure to get everyone into a light, party mood. As all the work can be done well in advance, the dish makes a sensible first, or main, course – and the mess at table is minimal.

cleaning the prawns, then 15 minutes

Serves 4–6
900 g/2 lb raw prawns in their shells, defrosted if frozen
50–75 g/2–3 oz butter
6–9 teaspoons freshly squeezed lemon juice

Pull the legs – and heads, if still on – away from the prawns but leave the body and tail shells attached to the meat. Wash the prawns in cold water and drain well.

Cut out 6 × 25 cm/10 in, or 4 × 30 cm/12 in, squares of foil. Divide the prawns, butter and lemon juice between the centres of each square and fold the sides to make loose parcels, then fold up the edges to seal tightly. Put the parcels on a baking sheet. They are now ready for the oven, which should be preheated to 190°C/375°F/gas 5 when you are ready to cook them. Bake for 10 minutes, and serve immediately.

Let each person open his parcel at the table on a large serving plate, and provide bowls or a communal soup plate to put the pretty shells in. Finger bowls, with warm water and a slice of lemon, are also a sensible idea.

- For a French accent, add 1 teaspoon Pernod or another kind of pastis to each parcel before cooking.
- If feeling in a Mexican mood, divide a small, finely chopped onion and 1 tablespoon bruised coriander seeds among the parcels with the butter and lemon juice.

Dipping Sauces for Prawns en Papillote

Having an array of differently flavoured, low-fat sauces for dipping will also delight. Make them a day ahead and chill to let the flavours develop, but serve them at room temperature. With such sauces omit the butter in the parcels and use only lemon, lime or orange juice to let people really enjoy your low-fat magic. Suggestions for your array might include 125–175 g/4–6 oz plain, Greek-style yoghurt mixed with each of the following:

- 1 teaspoon freshly grated root ginger, 1 teaspoon mustard seeds (preferably black for prettiness), 1 tablespoon lemon juice (in addition to that in the parcels) and freshly ground black pepper.
- 1 tablespoon orange – preferably blood orange – juice, plus 1 tablespoon chopped coriander leaves.
- 3 tablespoons chopped watercress leaves, plus 1 tablespoon lemon juice.
- 2 tablespoons chopped fresh basil leaves, plus 1 tablespoon lemon juice.
- ½–1 small crushed garlic clove.

Other dipping ideas for prawns are:

- Spicy red sauce made by mixing 125 g/4 oz tomato ketchup with 2 teaspoons creamed horseradish, 1 tablespoon lemon juice and freshly ground black pepper.
- Remoulade sauce (page 41).
- Red, yellow or green pepper sauce (page 99).
- Low-fat tartar sauce made by mixing 2 teaspoons chopped gherkins, 4 teaspoons finely chopped onion and 1 tablespoon lemon juice into 175 g/6 oz plain, Greek-style yoghurt.

BAKED BLACK MUSHROOMS AND COD

Like all the best recipes, this one is a crowd pleaser as well as being versatile. Make it with turbot, halibut or any other white fish, and with other kinds of soaked dried mushrooms such as wood ears, oyster mushrooms or ceps. As the quantities and method remain the same, it's quite fun to try different fish-mushroom combinations.

1¼ hours

Serves 4
50 g/2 oz Chinese dried mushrooms (page 10)
4 × 175–225 g/6–8 oz cod steaks
150 ml/¼ pint dry white wine
2 tablespoons olive or other polyunsaturated oil

For the fumet (fish stock)
2 fish heads or 225 g/8 oz fish bones, rinsed clean of all blood
2 fennel seeds
small handful of celery or lovage leaves
1 clove
3 black peppercorns

For serving
boiled rice

First make the fish stock by putting all the stock ingredients in a saucepan and covering with about 1.7 litres/3 pints cold water. Bring to the boil, then reduce the heat and simmer for 20–30 minutes. Strain the stock, discard the solids, and reduce the liquid to about 275 ml/½ pint by hard boiling. Put the stock aside to cool (see below).

Meanwhile, cover the mushrooms with hot water and let them soak for about 30 minutes until they are soft. Squeeze out the extra water and cut away the tough, inedible stem.

Heat the oven to 180°C/375°F/gas 5. Layer the mushroom caps between the fish steaks in a soufflé or other deep, ovenproof dish, large enough for the fish to fit in snugly. Whisk the wine and oil together and pour over the fish. Add just enough of the cooled fish stock to barely cover the steaks. The amount needed will vary according to the thickness of the fish and size of the dish, so add extra white wine or water if necessary.

Place the dish in the hot oven and cook for 25–30 minutes, or until the fish flakes easily with a fork. Serve the fish and mushrooms with boiled rice, spooning over some of the delicious cooking liquid.

SMOKED MACKEREL WITH RUM AND LIME

So heavenly is this dish, it could be called 'Holy mackerel'. Except that its inspiration came in a bar in Manhattan when I tasted a friend's rum soda with lime . . .

5 minutes, then 2–3 hours marinating, plus 15 minutes

Serves 4
    4 × 450 g/1 lb mackerel, cleaned, heads and tails removed
    8 tablespoons freshly squeezed lime juice (about 6 large limes)
    225 ml/8 fl oz dark rum

For garnish
    thin round slices of lime
    fresh mint sprigs

For serving
    Steamed fennel with pepper rings and mint (page 158)

Cut the mackerel across into 4 cm/1½ in steaks. Pour the lime and rum into a shallow dish to mix, then place the steaks in one layer in the liquid. Refrigerate the steaks, turning them over in the marinade every 30 minutes, for 2–3 hours.

Shake off the excess liquid but don't dry the mackerel steaks, reserve the marinade and position the fish on the rack of your home smoker, out of doors. Light the spirit burners under the device and leave the fish to smoke for 10 minutes or until they feel just firm when pressed with the finger.

Transfer the steaks to serving plates, pour 1–2 tablespoons of the marinade over each serving and garnish with the lime slices and mint sprigs, if wished. Serve right away with the steamed fennel.

HALIBUT POACHED IN VEGETABLE-HERB SAUCE

This useful sauce gives a beautiful flavour to poached white fish steaks. And halibut steaks are among the finest. So – a perfect combination.

35 minutes

Serves 4
    4 tablespoons polyunsaturated oil
    2 large onions, chopped
    2 medium-sized carrots, grated
    2–3 celery stalks, chopped
    400 ml/14 fl oz canned tomatoes

150 ml/¼ pint dry white wine
5–6 fresh basil leaves, chopped, or 1 teaspoon dried basil
25 g/1 oz parsley, stems discarded, then roughly chopped
1–2 spring onions, chopped
2 garlic cloves, finely chopped
salt (optional) and freshly ground black pepper
900 g/2 lb halibut fillet, in one piece, skinned, then cut into 8 thick
    slices

For serving
boiled rice

Heat the oil in a large heavy-based saucepan, or a flameproof casserole, over a low heat. When hot, add the onions and let them cook until they begin to soften. Stir in the carrots and celery, cover, and leave to sweat for 3–4 minutes, stirring occasionally.

Add the tomatoes (and their juices), pressing against the sides of the pan with a wooden spoon to lightly crush them, then add the wine, basil, parsley, spring onions and garlic, and stir together. Bring the mixture to the boil, reduce the heat and simmer for 5 minutes. Season with salt, if wished, and freshly ground black pepper. Add the fish slices to the pan and, spreading some sauce over each one, bring to the boil, then cover and cook over a low heat for 6 minutes.

Turn the fish in the sauce, cover and cook for a further 6–8 minutes or until the fish feels firm to the touch and will flake easily. Serve at once with boiled rice.

CREOLE PRAWNS

Quick, simple, and a favourite dish since childhood, this will certainly see me into a healthy – and well-fed – old age.

30 minutes

Serves 4
    3 tablespoons polyunsaturated oil
    1 large onion, chopped
    1 garlic clove, finely chopped
    1 smallish green pepper, seeded and chopped

a few fresh rosemary sprigs, bruised, or a large pinch of dried
  rosemary
2 bay leaves, crumbled
1 celery stalk, trimmed and finely chopped
salt (optional) and freshly ground black pepper
400 g/14 oz canned tomatoes
450 g/1 lb shelled prawns, defrosted if frozen, rinsed and drained

For serving
boiled rice

Heat the oil in a saucepan over a low heat, add the onion, garlic and
pepper, and cook until the onion is soft but not browned, stirring
occasionally. Add the rosemary, bay leaves, celery, and salt and pepper
to taste, then stir in the canned tomatoes, breaking them up with a
spoon. Bring the mixture to a simmer, then cook very gently for 15–20
minutes.

Stir the prawns into the sauce just to heat through or, if necessary, to
cook them until just firm. Do not overcook. Immediately serve the
creole mixture over boiled rice.

- Monkfish or red snapper fillets cut into bite-sized pieces taste delicious
  cooked this way. Though they will need cooking a little longer than
  prawns, be careful not to overcook.

TUNA WITH FLAGEOLETS

My favourite beans, flageolets, have a delicate texture, with the merest
hint of sweetness about them, no doubt because they are harvested
while still young and tender. Fresh tuna is hard to find but when you do,
grill it lightly as I do below and serve it with flageolets. When it isn't
available from my wonderful fishmonger, I rely on tuna packed in
water. And when my larder is low on flageolets, haricot beans do nicely.

This is one of the very few dishes that I feel is improved by a little salt.
My favourite salt is from Maldon, on the Essex coast, and it comes in the
form of pretty flakes, so I know how much I'm using. Each time I eat
one of the salt flakes, my delicious tuna and flageolets take on a new, and
delightful, dimension.

Overnight soaking, plus 3½–4 hours, then 10 minutes

Serves 4
    350 g/12 oz dried flageolet beans, picked over
    4 × 175–225 g/6–8 oz tuna steaks, boned, or fillets of an even
       thickness
    olive oil
    salt (optional) and freshly ground black pepper
    1–2 lemons

Soak the beans overnight in plenty of water to cover. Drain and put the beans in a large saucepan, cover well with fresh water and bring to the boil. Simmer for about 3–4 hours, skimming after 1 hour and topping up the pan with boiling water as necessary. When tender, drain the flageolets and let them cool, stirring occasionally.

Heat the grill to high. Put the fish steaks or fillets on a lightly greased baking sheet, and place about 5 cm/2 in under the grill. Cook for about 2 minutes, then turn the fish over and replace under the grill. Check again after 1 minute, and thereafter at 30 second intervals. The fish is done when it feels just firm but not hard. Given the difference in thickness of the fish, grills, and how people like their fish, it's impossible to be more precise! I like my fish lightly pink and moist; you may well prefer yours better done, and less moist. But by remembering how you like your cooked fish to 'feel', you've taken a giant step towards becoming a good fish cook.

Back to the recipe. Transfer the fish to warm serving plates and spoon some of the flageolets in a pretty portion on each of the plates. Dribble about 1 tablespoon olive oil over the beans, add a little salt, if wished, then grind on some pepper. Liberally squeeze lemon juice all over the fish and serve.

HONEY-MUSTARD SALMON EN PAPILLOTE

An odd combination this may seem, but a luscious one it is!

20 minutes

Serves 4
    25 g/1 oz unsalted butter, plus extra for greasing
    4 × 225 g/8 oz boneless salmon steaks, skin removed
    juice of 1 medium-sized lemon
    150 g/5 oz plain, Greek-style yoghurt

2 tablespoons runny honey
1 tablespoon Meaux or similar coarse-grained mustard
2 tablespoons pine nuts, lightly toasted under the grill
1 garlic clove, crushed
2 tablespoons chopped fresh dill
2 tablespoons freshly grated Parmesan cheese

For serving
tossed mixed salad

Heat the oven to 220°C/425°F/gas 7. Prepare four sheets of foil, 30 × 38 cm/12 × 15 in and grease them lightly with butter. Put a salmon steak in the centre of each sheet and set aside.

Mix together the lemon, yoghurt, honey, mustard, pine nuts, garlic, dill and Parmesan and spread an equal amount over the top of each steak, then dot with the butter cut into small bits. Fold the foil over twice to join the edges tightly. Place the parcels on a baking tray and cook in the oven for 8 minutes or until the fish feels firm when touched.

Transfer the parcels to warmed serving plates and serve immediately with a tossed mixed salad, letting each person open his own parcel to fully enjoy the fragrance.

SCALLOP AND PRAWN MOUSSELINE

Mousselines for me are a frequent treat since I discovered how to make them without cream, and they are so *simple*! This one is especially good as an elegant starter, or for a light lunch or supper when you need a little culinary cosseting. Store them in the refrigerator up to 2 days ahead; the flavour just improves.

20 minutes plus chilling, then 30 minutes, plus cooling and chilling

Serves 2–4
   225–275 g/8–10 oz scallops, defrosted if frozen, and cleaned, (the
      pink corals reserved for the cat)
   125 g/4 oz raw prawns, peeled
   8 tablespoons egg white
   salt (optional) and freshly ground white pepper
   125 g/8 oz plain, Greek-style yoghurt
   ¼ teaspoon lime or lemon juice

about 1 tablespoon snipped chives
softened butter for greasing

For garnish
lime or lemon wedges
a few chives, snipped into 25 mm/1 in lengths
pale green lettuce salad

Put the shellfish into a food processor fitted with a metal blade and
blend for 10 seconds or until the mixture becomes a purée. Add the egg
white, a little seasoning and process several more seconds to mix.

Add the yoghurt and lime or lemon juice to the purée and process
again until the mixture is slightly thick, but don't over-process. Fold in
the snipped chives and check the seasoning. Cover and refrigerate for 30
minutes to 2 hours.

Meanwhile, grease 4 × 5 fl oz dariole moulds with softened butter.
Cut 4 circles of greaseproof paper to fit the bottoms of the moulds. Put
them in place and grease lightly. Heat the oven to 170°C/325°F/gas 3.

Spoon the purée into the moulds. Tap the bottoms of the moulds to
eliminate air bubbles and smooth the tops of the mousselines with a
knife. Cover the top of each mould with foil and put them in a small
roasting pan. Fill the pan halfway up with boiling water and bake for 25
minutes.

Remove the moulds from the water and let them cool, then refrigerate 6 hours or overnight. Loosen the mousselines by running the tip of a
thin knife around the inside edge of the moulds. Turn the mousselines
out onto small serving plates, remove the greaseproof paper and garnish
with a little salad composed mainly of the small, pale inner leaves of
lettuces.

- If fresh chives aren't available, there are other lovely ingredients you can
  use instead, such as the finely chopped green tops of spring onions, 1–1½
  teaspoons freeze-dried pink peppercorns, roughly crushed, or ½ teaspoon good dried tarragon. Be inventive; just remember the relative
  strength of flavour when adding your substitutions.

STEAMED COD WITH FRESH TOMATO SAUCE

Richness and flavour is given to this beautifully light dish by the
Italian-style sauce, mixed with thick yoghurt. Just the thing for a rainy
day, a sunny day, or any day . . .

1–1¼ hours

Serves 6
  juice of 2–3 fresh lemons
  6 × 175–225 g/6–8 oz boned cod, halibut or other white fish steaks,
    skin discarded
  unsalted butter for greasing

For the tomato and yoghurt sauce
  450 g/1 lb canned tomatoes, drained
  1 shallot, finely chopped, or 1 tablespoon finely chopped onion
  1 garlic clove, crushed
  1 teaspoon tomato purée
  freshly ground black pepper
  225 g/8 oz plain, Greek-style yoghurt, at room temperature
  salt (optional)

For garnish
  lumpfish caviar (black), or chopped parsley

First make the sauce. Discard the seeds from the canned tomatoes, then put them into a heavy-based saucepan with the shallot or onion, garlic, tomato purée and freshly ground black pepper. Cook over a medium-low heat for 5–6 minutes, stirring occasionally and breaking the tomatoes up with a spoon. Cover, remove the pan from the heat and leave for 10 minutes, to allow the flavours to develop.

Strain the sauce through a sieve into a clean pan and simmer gently to reduce it until the mixture is very thick. Remove the pan from the heat and stir in the yoghurt. Taste and add salt, if wished. Keep warm by putting the pan over another filled with hot water, but don't let the upper pan actually rest in the water.

Squeeze lemon juice over the fish steaks, wrap them together loosely in muslin, then put them in a lightly greased steamer or on a greased trivet above, not in, bubbling water. Cover and let the fish steam for about 5 minutes or until the flesh feels firm but not hard to the touch. Immediately remove the steamer or trivet from the water and set the fish aside. Divide the sauce between 6 hot serving plates, then place a fish steak in the middle of each plate. Garnish with the caviar, if wished, or with chopped parsley and serve immediately.

POACHED MONKFISH WITH ROQUEFORT DRESSING

This IS a low-fat cookery book; Jack has not abandoned us, even though the dressing for the delicately cooked fish is strongly flavoured with blue cheese. The magic is that you only need about 1 tablespoon of Roquefort for the dressing, because what fat content there is in the thick yoghurt absorbs the cheese's magnificent flavour. The principle of fats absorbing other flavours can work to our advantage in many dishes, especially if we are provident and allow the yoghurt enough time to take on the desired flavour.

1–2 days flavouring the yoghurt, making the court-bouillon, then about 10 minutes

Serves 4
  juice of 1 lemon
  700–900 g/1½–2 lb monkfish or other firm white fish fillets
  400 g/14 oz canned artichoke hearts in water, drained

For the Roquefort dressing
  15 g/½ oz Roquefort or other strongly flavoured blue cheese
  225 g/8 oz plain, Greek-style yoghurt

For the court-bouillon
  1 large onion, sliced
  3 medium-sized celery stalks chopped
  2 bay leaves, crumbled
  1 medium-sized carrot, sliced into rounds
  2 parsley sprigs
  6 peppercorns
  1 teaspoon coriander seeds
  275 ml/½ pint dry white wine

For garnish
  4 small bay leaves
  1 teaspoon coriander seeds

Make the dressing at least one, and preferably two, days before serving the dish, crumble the cheese finely with a fork and stir it into the yoghurt. Cover the container well and refrigerate.

About 1 hour before serving, remove the flavoured yoghurt from the refrigerator to let it come to room temperature. To prepare the court-bouillon, fill a large saucepan with all the bouillon ingredients, add 1.1 litre/2 pints water and bring to the boil, then reduce the heat, cover and simmer gently for 20–30 minutes. Strain the mixture through a sieve and reserve the liquid. If you wish to make the court-bouillon in advance, then strain, cool, cover and refrigerate it until you cook the fish.

Heat the oven to 180°C/350°F/gas 4. Pour the court-bouillon into a small roasting tin, squeeze in the lemon juice and put the tin in the oven. When it is very hot but before starting to evaporate, add the fish fillets, topping up the liquid with a little boiling water to just cover the fish if necessary. Cook in the oven for 4–6 minutes or until the fish flakes easily when tested with a fork.

Immediately remove the fish from the court-bouillon with a fish slice, transferring it to a warmed serving dish. Garnish it with the bay leaves, sprinkle over the coriander seeds and spoon a little of the blue cheese sauce on the fish, serving the rest separately.

- For an excellent cold version, cook the fish earlier in the day, let it cool to room temperature, chill until ready to serve, then garnish and serve with chilled blue cheese dressing. Very good.
- The blue cheese dressing is so delicious that I tend to flavour several containers of yoghurt, then I can also enjoy the pleasure of eating it with new potatoes, raw vegetables, cold meats, shellfish – and on its own.

POULTRY

CHICKEN SUPREMES WITH YELLOW AND RED PEPPER SAUCES
Chicken supremes with green pepper-sherry sauce
Yellow or red pepper-yoghurt soup

CHICKEN SUPREMES GRILLED WITH GREEN PEPPERCORNS
Chicken supremes grilled with pine nut sauce
Cutting your own supremes

RICOTTA KIEV
Boning chicken breast joints

COQ AU RIESLING

COQ AU VIN MAIGRE
Trotter stock

CHICKEN WITH ARTICHOKE HEARTS

TERRINE SUPREME
Herb vinaigrette

CHICKEN, WATERCRESS AND RADISH SALAD

CHICKEN AND SWEET GHERKIN SALAD
Tomatoes stuffed with chicken and sweet gherkin salad
How to make sweet pickled gherkins

CHICKEN BRICK COOKING

APPLE-BRAISED GUINEA FOWL
Apple-braised pheasant

CRYSTAL-COOKED POUSSIN WITH FIG-MUSTARD SAUCE

GLAZED POACHED CHICKEN WITH TWO STUFFINGS
How to bone a chicken

TURKEY STROGANOFF

TURKEY TONNATO
How to bone a turkey breast

GRILLED DUCK WITH BIGARADE SAUCE

DUCK IN POMEGRANATE-WALNUT SAUCE

SMOKED CHICKEN WITH TOMATO VINAIGRETTE (see *Sauces*)

Singularly versatile, inexpensive and widely available, chicken's eminence as *the* low-fat meat seems assured. It has been successfully flavoured, stuffed, basted or garnished with almost every other food possible, and it can be cooked in myriad ways. The only taboos, from the low-fat point of view, are frying and traditional roasting – due to the amount of fat its dry meat needs to absorb in order to be 'done' to a succulent turn.

If the family threaten a lynching unless you produce a roast chicken, there is a sneaky solution: a chicken brick. Put a whole dressed bird – no additions – into the earthenware brick and, once cooked, pour off the melted fat and enjoy the pure chicken juices as a gravy. Other alternatives are to poach, braise, simmer, grill or home-smoke chicken, or any bird with little or no fat.

Poultry meat is generally very lean. The fatty culprit lies in the skin and the thin white layer just underneath it, and these are easily sacrificed. For instance, chicken contains about 5 per cent fat in its flesh, and light turkey meat 1 per cent (the dark meat about 4 per cent). By the same token, duck – bereft of all its skin and fatty pockets – has superbly flavoured lean meat containing only 9–10 per cent fat. Roast duck, on the other hand, with its admittedly scrumptious crispy skin – and all the fat *that* contains – is nearly three times as high in fat, about 29 per cent.

CHICKEN SUPREMES WITH YELLOW AND RED PEPPER SAUCES

Though nobody will spurn the sauces even if they have been made just before the meal, the longer ahead you can prepare them, the better the taste will be. Just remember not to sample too much while letting the flavours develop, or you won't have any left.

15 minutes, plus 1–2 days chilling, then 10 minutes

Serves 6
   6 boned chicken breasts (supremes) with the wing joints attached
      (page 101), trimmed of any fat
   polyunsaturated oil, for greasing
   freshly ground black pepper

For the pepper sauces
   1 large yellow pepper
   1 large red pepper
   2 garlic cloves, chopped
   2 teaspoons dry sherry
   2 teaspoons medium-sweet sherry
   425 ml/¾ pint thick, Greek-style yoghurt

For garnish
   6 watercress sprigs

For serving
   cos lettuce
   tomatoes
   chopped fresh mint
   lemon juice

Eight hours to two days before cooking the chicken, make the sauces. Spear the peppers through their stems on large forks and turn them over a gas flame or under a hot grill until the skin burns on all sides, about 5 minutes.

Hold a pepper under cold, not too violently, running water and, when cool enough to handle, rub off the charred skin. Repeat with the second pepper.

Slice the tops off each pepper, then discard the uncharred top, stem, seeds and ribs. Chop the yellow pepper and put in a food processor, or blender, with half the chopped garlic and the dry sherry. Blend the mixture to a purée. Strain through a sieve, saving the delicious liquid for soup, and reserve the purée. Repeat the process with the red pepper and the medium-sweet sherry.

Divide the yoghurt between 2 bowls, then stir the yellow pepper purée into one bowl, the red purée into the second. Cover well and refrigerate up to 2 days.

Thirty minutes to one hour before cooking, remove the sauces from the refrigerator.

Heat the grill to high. Put the chicken breasts on a greased baking sheet and grill for 2–3 minutes each side or until the flesh feels just firm, but still juicy to the touch.

Transfer the chicken to serving plates. Spoon a ribbon of both sauces over each chicken breast, then position a sprig of watercress beside each breast, tucking the stem underneath the chicken, to garnish. Grind over a little black pepper and serve with a salad of shredded cos leaves, sliced tomatoes and chopped mint with a lemon juice dressing.

- Green pepper with dry sherry also makes a delicious sauce, but the colours, and perhaps the flavours, of sweet yellow and pungent red peppers are more dramatic. But even a green pepper sauce on its own is delicious, and pretty, with, say, poached salmon!
- The pepper sauces thinned with extra yoghurt – plain, but not necessarily thick – make a very smart chilled soup.

CHICKEN SUPREMES GRILLED WITH GREEN PEPPERCORNS

Good butchers sell boned, skinned chicken breasts, or will even bone and skin a chicken breast quarter for you (ask for the wing and rib bones for stock), but it is easy to cut your own supremes, leaving the first wing joint attached for extra elegance.

For salads, composite dishes and stock (page 37), I buy whole chickens and bone the breasts myself, cutting them as supremes, then wrap them, individually, in cling film and pack them together in a freezer bag. When there are four or more of them, it's time for a dinner party supreme!

cutting the supremes, then about 10 minutes

Serves 2
   1 large chicken
   olive or other polyunsaturated oil, for greasing
   1 teaspoon freeze-dried green peppercorns, or green peppercorns in
      brine, drained and rinsed

To cut your own supremes, place the chicken, breast side up, with the
neck end towards you, on a work surface. Roll the skin back, then pull it
right off the chicken and discard. With a very sharp knife carefully trim
off any fat attached to the breast, then firmly take hold of one side of the
chicken. Run the knife blade along the length of one side of the
breastbone, carefully cutting and scraping downwards against the rib
cage. Trim around any small bones at the bottom to free the flesh, then
slice through the tendons that attach the wing to the carcass. After a
couple of attempts you will master the technique easily and perform the
operation in less than 30 seconds.
   Cut round and through the skin and flesh at the top of the first wing
joint, then give a tug and pull the rest of the wing away. Discard any
skin remaining on the little 'mock drumstick' attached to the boned
breast, then cut the supreme on the other side of the chicken. Cut away
the thigh and leg portions, if wished, to use in other dishes, discard the
skin and any visible fat, then make stock with the rest of the carcass
(pages 37–8).
   Heat the grill to high. Put the supremes, cut-sides up, on a lightly
greased baking tray and brush with oil. When the grill is really hot,
position the supremes about 5 cm/2 in under the heat and cook for
2–2½ minutes. Turn them over and brush with oil. Spread the peppercorns, lightly crushed if freeze-dried, over the meat and put back under
the heat for 2½–3 minutes or until the supremes are just firm but not
dry. They should be very succulent, look and taste a treat, and be served
right away.

   • A pretty idea for Christmas, or any other, time is to use a mixture of pink
     and green peppercorns as above.
   • For a pine nut sauce, while the supremes grill, fry 50 g/2 oz nuts in 3
     tablespoons olive oil over a low heat, stirring occasionally. When most of
     the nuts are browned, but not burned, remove from the heat and pour
     over the supremes.
   • For pomegranate-walnut sauce to serve with the supremes, see pages
     120–1.
   • For tomato sauce to serve with the supremes, see pages 166–7
   • The above recipes are also suitable – and quite delicious – with chicken
     thighs, or duck breasts and leg-thigh joints.

RICOTTA KIEV

Gone are the days when I could eat chicken Kiev, filled with melted seasoned butter, or worse, buttery goose liver pâté. My low-fat regime absolutely prohibits such pleasures, but chicken Kiev with a low-fat, herby filling is very permissible.

If you want to prepare the Kievs a week ahead, as I often do, you must use fresh chickens (or chicken breasts), as repeated thawing and freezing can encourage bacterial growth and could be dangerous. If you do freeze the prepared Kievs, be sure to defrost them, slowly and completely, in the refrigerator, then use them promptly.

30–45 minutes preparing the Kievs, then 10 minutes

Serves 6
  6 skinned, boned chicken breasts (see below)
  175 g/6 oz fresh Ricotta cheese
  2–3 tablespoons chopped fresh herbs such as tarragon, sage,
      parsley, chervil and dill or a mixture, or 2–3 teaspoons mixed
      dried herbs
  1 small garlic clove, crushed (optional)
  lemon juice
  75–125 g/3–4 oz flour
  75–125 g/3–4 oz dry breadcrumbs
  3 medium-sized egg whites
  salt (optional) and freshly ground black pepper
  polyunsaturated oil, for deep frying

Moisten two sheets of greaseproof paper or cling film and put a chicken breast between the wetted sides. Using a rolling pin or meat bat, flatten the meat by striking it with even blows, using less force on the narrow ends. The flatter the meat, the better, so remoisten the paper, if necessary, to help prevent the meat tearing. Repeat with the other pieces, then set aside.

Stir together the fresh Ricotta, herbs, garlic and a little lemon juice to taste. Spoon some of the mixture over each breast, placing it nearest the wider end. Lay the small piece of chicken (the fillet), usually attached to the breast but which sometimes comes off separately once boned, over the filling, lengthways, and fold the sides of the breast together. Secure the two sides with small skewers or wooden cocktail sticks. Repeat with the other chicken pieces.

Spread the flour and breadcrumbs over separate soup, or large serving, plates and lightly beat the egg whites in another soup plate. Mix salt, if wished, and pepper into the flour, then roll each piece of meat in it to coat. Then dip into the egg white, roll in breadcrumbs and put aside. Repeat with the remaining pieces. You can now either wrap them individually and freeze; cover and refrigerate up to 2 hours; or cook them right away.

Pour oil into a large, deep pan to a depth of about 5 cm/2 in and heat to 190°C/375°F or until a cube of stale bread will brown in 50 seconds. Lower the chicken breasts carefully, one at a time, into the hot oil, giving the oil a little time to reheat before adding the next one. (You may have to cook them in batches of 2–3 if your pan is not large enough. Keep warm in a low oven, if necessary.) When deep golden-brown all over, about 5 minutes, remove the chicken, drain well on absorbent paper, take out the skewers, if wished, and serve right away.

- If you buy your chicken breasts as joints, you can easily bone them yourself by using a very sharp knife to cut away the meat, always keeping the blade against the bone, gently pulling back the meat as you cut. Snip through the wing joint, if necessary, to remove the wing.

COQ AU RIESLING

When you pine for good coq au vin but haven't time, make coq au Riesling.

1 hour

Serves 4
    25 g/1 oz butter
    1 large onion, finely chopped
    4 chicken quarters, each cut into 2 pieces with all visible fat
       removed
    225 g/8 oz mushrooms, wiped with a damp cloth, and sliced
    275 ml/½ pint Riesling, or other dry white wine
    salt (optional) and freshly ground white pepper
    125 g/4 oz plain, Greek-style yoghurt, stirred

For garnish
chopped parsley

Melt the butter in a large, heavy-bottomed saucepan, or frying pan with a lid, over a low heat. Stir in the onion, cover and cook for 5 minutes. Add the chicken, cover, raise the heat slightly and cook for 15 minutes, then add the mushrooms, wine and season with salt, if wished, and pepper. Cover and cook for 25 minutes.

Transfer the meat to a warmed serving dish and keep warm. Reduce the cooking liquid by half over a medium heat, then stir in the yoghurt.

Pour the sauce over the chicken, sprinkle with parsley and serve immediately.

COQ AU VIN MAIGRE

Somehow the French name sounds better than 'low-fat chicken in red wine', but, whatever the language, the stew tastes just as good. The flavour of the wine is essential to this dish, especially as it is low-fat, so use a goodish wine – one you wouldn't mind drinking with a nice main course – such as this.

Making the stock, plus 3 hours marinating, then 50 minutes

Serves 4
    1 pig's trotter, preferably split in half lengthways
    425 ml/¾ pint dry red wine
    1 medium-sized onion, halved and sliced
    1 bouquet garni
    6 black peppercorns
    4 chicken quarters, skin and any visible fat removed
    16–20 pickling onions, peeled but left whole
    4 tablespoons olive oil
    350 g/12 oz button mushrooms, wiped with a damp cloth and stems
        discarded
    1 garlic clove, chopped
    salt (optional) and freshly ground black pepper

To make a jellied stock from the pig's trotter, start a day or two before you want to use it. Put the trotter in a large saucepan and cover with cold water. Put the pan over a very low heat. The water will slowly come to a simmer, about 1½–2 hours, while the trotter's flavour and gelatine flow out into the water. Raise the heat very slightly and cook for 2–6 hours, skimming and topping up with boiling water as necessary. The longer you can let the stock gently cook, the more flavour and jelly it will contain. Cool the trotter, strip off the meat in large pieces, cover and refrigerate, then discard the rest of the trotter. Reduce the stock by rapid boiling to about 575 ml/1 pint. Cool, strain, cover and refrigerate. Remove all traces of fat from the top of the jellied stock before using.

Put the wine, sliced onion, bouquet garni and peppercorns into a saucepan, bring to the boil, then simmer for 2–3 minutes. Remove the pan from the heat, pour the liquid into a shallow bowl and let it cool. Cut each chicken quarter into two, and put into the wine. Leave 3 or more hours, turning the pieces occasionally in the marinade.

Bring a pan of water to the boil, add the pickling onions, blanch for 2 minutes, then drain well and leave them to cool. Remove the chicken pieces from the marinade and dry on absorbent paper. Strain and reserve the marinade and the bouquet garni. Heat the oil in a flameproof casserole, or heavy-based frying pan, over a medium heat, add the chicken and brown it quickly on all sides. Remove the chicken from the pan and reserve.

Heat the oven to 200°C/400°F/gas 6. Add the pickling onions to the pan and cook, stirring occasionally, until they begin to brown, then remove and set aside. Reduce the heat slightly, add the mushrooms and cook, stirring occasionally, until tender. Transfer the mushrooms to a dish and reserve. Pour away the liquid in the pan, then wipe it clean with kitchen paper.

Return the chicken, onions and mushrooms to the pan, add the marinade, bouquet garni, garlic, half the jellied stock and the meat from the trotter. Refrigerate, or label and freeze, the rest of the stock to use in another dish. Bring the mixture to the boil, then transfer, if necessary, to a casserole, cover and cook in the oven for 15 minutes. Turn the pieces over in the liquid, cover and continue cooking for a further 15 minutes or until the meat is tender.

Transfer the chicken, onions, mushrooms and pork to a warmed serving dish and keep warm while you boil the liquid rapidly to reduce and thicken it. Taste, add salt, if wished, and pepper, and spoon the sauce over the chicken. Serve at once.

- Trotter stock has much to commend it, as, in addition to the stock, you get enough meltingly good meat to serve 2, perhaps with remoulade sauce (page 41), or to serve 3 in a composite dish. The reduced, skimmed stock freezes well, ready to add richness and flavour to many a soup or stew.

CHICKEN WITH ARTICHOKE HEARTS

A simple dish loaded with flavour, this will easily satisfy family and the fussiest of guests.

1 hour

Serves 4
    4 chicken quarters
    4 tablespoons olive or other polyunsaturated oil
    150 ml/¼ pint dry white wine
    2 large onions, sliced into thin rounds
    4 medium-sized tomatoes, blanched, skinned and cut into quarters
    425 g/15 oz canned artichoke hearts, drained and quartered
    2 teaspoons coriander seeds, lightly crushed
    salt (optional) and freshly ground black pepper

To garnish
flat-leaved parsley, stems discarded
8–12 low-fat croûtons (page 175)

Remove the skin and any visible fat from the chicken quarters, then joint into legs, thighs, breasts and wings. Put half the oil in a large heavy-based saucepan, or flameproof casserole, over a medium heat. When hot, add the chicken, a few pieces at a time, browning lightly on all sides, then setting aside while browning the rest. Return all the chicken joints to the pan, putting the breasts and wings on top. Add the wine, bring to the boil, then reduce the heat to a very gentle simmer, cover and cook for 30 minutes, adding a little water, or extra wine, if necessary, after about 20 minutes. The meat should be very tender.

Transfer the chicken to a warmed serving dish, covering it with foil to keep warm. Skim any fat from the surface of the cooking liquid, then bring to the boil to reduce and thicken slightly. Remove from the heat.

Heat the rest of the oil in a small saucepan over a medium-low heat, add the onions and cook, stirring frequently, until they begin to soften. Stir in the tomatoes, chopped artichoke hearts and coriander seeds, then cover and cook over a low heat for 5 minutes or until the tomatoes soften. Spread the mixture over the chicken. Reheat the reduced liquid and pour it over the chicken, garnish with a little parsley, sprinkle over the croûtons and serve.

TERRINE SUPREME

Perfection on the plate, and magic to taste. Fresh herbs, boned chicken breasts and thin slices of bacon combine in this glorious terrine. It's a treasure you can make ahead, then serve at leisure for lunch, as a starter, or an elegant supper à deux.

1½ hours, plus cooling and overnight chilling

Serves 6–8
    25 g/1 oz parsley, stems discarded
    15–25 g/½–1 oz fresh basil leaves
    15–25 g/½–1 oz fresh tarragon leaves
    15–25 g/½–1 oz fresh chervil leaves
    5 medium-sized or large boned chicken breasts (page 101)
    unsalted butter, for greasing
    12 thin rashers lean back bacon, trimmed of all fat
    225 g/8 oz plain, Greek-style yoghurt
    3 medium-sized egg whites

For the herb vinaigrette
    1 tablespoon chopped parsley
    1 tablespoon chopped fresh basil leaves
    1 tablespoon chopped fresh tarragon leaves
    1 tablespoon chopped fresh chervil leaves
    175/225 ml/6–8 fl oz olive oil
    4–6 tablespoons white wine vinegar

Finely chop the parsley, basil, tarragon and chervil together, then put aside. Wet one chicken breast with cold water and place between 2 sheets of cling film on a work surface. Hit it firmly, and repeatedly, with a rolling pin or meat bat to flatten to about 3 mm/⅛ in thick, rewetting the cling film frequently to prevent the meat tearing. Flatten the other breasts. Heat the oven to 190°C/375°F/gas 5.

Grease a 900 g/2 lb loaf tin with butter and put in one of the flattened chicken breasts, spreading it out and using the fillet strip (attached to the back of the breast) to help cover as much of the bottom of the tin as possible. Then make a layer with 2 bacon rashers on top of the chicken. Don't fret if there are a few gaps between the pieces of meat; the yoghurt will seep through to fill any spaces and the flavour will be just as good. Sprinkle over a layer of chopped herbs, then repeat with layers of chicken, bacon and herbs, finishing with chicken.

Whisk the yoghurt and egg whites together and pour into the tin, lifting the meat gently away from the sides to allow the yoghurt to fill the tin. Put the loaf tin in a small roasting pan in the oven and fill the roasting pan with boiling water, to come halfway up the sides of the loaf tin. Cook in the oven for 1 hour, then remove the loaf tin from the water and leave to cool to room temperature.

Cover the tin with foil, then put on a large plate to catch any juices. Weight a plate and press on top of the terrine; refrigerate overnight. Or, to help press the terrine evenly, put another 900 g/2 lb loaf tin on top of the foil, just inside the rim of the lower tin, and place the weights inside the upper tin.

The next day, unmould the terrine by running a knife around its edges, then turn it out onto a serving plate. Whisk together the herb vinaigrette ingredients and serve 1–2 tablespoons of it with each slice of the lovely terrine.

CHICKEN, WATERCRESS AND RADISH SALAD

I do recommend this chicken salad. It is one of my favourites because it includes sharp-tasting watercress *and* radish leaves, which most innocents toss away. Unless it's the middle of winter, when I pine for radishes and will pay over the odds for even a handful of the trimmed red orbs, I do not buy radishes without leaves. Now these may be wilted, but as long as 'they ain't pest-eaten or yellow, I buy 'em'.

Once home, and here is the trick, I undo the bunch and let the radishes, with their leaves, have a good clean and soak in cold water with the spring onions, tomatoes and whatever else needs any after-shopping libation. Mine is a white wine spritzer. Then I gather the radishes together, give them a good shake, put them in a small bowl of water – roots in, perky green leaves sticking out – and store them in the refrigerator. For up to 2 days they stay fresh enough to sharpen my salads – a true boon, especially in early spring before other salad greens are available.

about 25 minutes

Serves 4
   4 chicken breasts
   425 ml/¾ pint chicken stock (page 37)
   large bunch of watercress
   bunch of smallish radishes with leaves, soaked

50 g/2 oz walnuts
1 teaspoon cider vinegar
freshly ground black pepper

Cut the wing joints away from the breasts and refrigerate or freeze for stock or another dish.

Pour the stock into a saucepan and bring to the boil, add the chicken breasts and boiling water just to cover. Reduce the heat until the water barely bubbles and leave the chicken to poach for 7–10 minutes depending on the thickness of the meat. It should be barely pink inside. Remove the chicken from the stock and let it cool.

Meanwhile, clean the watercress, discarding the stalks and thick stems but keeping the leaves whole. Shake the radishes dry, if necessary discard the roots, then cut off the leaves. Tear the leaves into bite-sized pieces and put in a serving bowl with the watercress. Slice the radishes and add to the bowl.

Bring the chicken stock to the boil, reduce it to about 150 ml/¼ pint and remove from the heat.

Meanwhile, strip the chicken off the bones, then tear the warm meat into fine, fine shreds or slice into very fine batons. Fold the chicken, with the walnuts, into the leaves and radishes.

Stir the vinegar into the stock and pour over the chicken. Grate on plenty of black pepper, toss well and serve.

CHICKEN AND SWEET GHERKIN SALAD

Chicken salad can be as ritzy or as simple as a cook wants to make it. I usually use leftover chicken for this, but the other elements add a deliciously distinctive tone.

2 days for the sweet pickled gherkins, then cooking the chicken, plus
    5 minutes

Serves 4
    450 g/1 lb cooked, boned chicken, skin and any fat discarded
    green tops of 2–4 spring onions, chopped, or 2–3 tablespoons fresh
        chives cut into 20–25 mm/¾–1 in lengths
    4 tablespoons coarsely chopped sweet pickled gherkins (see below)
    1 tablespoon freshly squeezed lemon juice

150 g/5 oz plain, Greek-style yoghurt
coarsely ground black pepper
salt (optional)

To serve
crisp lettuce leaves
thin slices of pumpernickel bread

Chop the chicken into bite-sized pieces and mix it in a bowl with the spring onions or chives and pickled gherkins. Stir the lemon juice into the yoghurt and pour into the bowl. Coarsely grind the pepper over the salad, mix well and taste. As the gherkins were originally pickled in brine, the mixture may not need added salt.

Serve with crisp lettuce leaves and pumpernickel bread.

- To make sweet pickled gherkins, drain a jar of pickled gherkins and cut the gherkins into rounds about 12 mm/½ in thick. Sprinkle a thick layer of granulated sugar into the jar, add a layer of gherkins, sprinkle over more sugar and repeat until all the gherkins are used, finishing with a layer of sugar. Cover tightly with the lid and refrigerate for 48 hours, laying the jar on its side and turning every 12 hours. Will keep indefinitely in the refrigerator.
- Try serving this mixture in tomatoes. Cut off the tomato tops, spoon out the seeds and fill with the chicken salad. Replace the lids, if wished, and chill briefly or serve immediately.

CHICKEN BRICK COOKING

Jack Sprat loves the ease and resulting flavour of baking – really braising – in inexpensive terracotta bricks, but he is appalled at the fatty cooking liquid which forms around a chicken. To all would-be svelte, healthy people he suggests that when next preparing a chicken, weigh it and remove the skin from all but the leg and wing tips. Then remove all the visible fat, or as much as a reasonable amount of time allows. Now weigh the fat and skin. You will probably find, as he did, that on a 1.7 kg/3¾ lb chicken, 500 g/18 oz of it is high calorie, downright dangerous fat and skin. The carcass, he found later, weighed 350 g/12 oz, so the meat – for which he had paid so much – was only half the weight of the bird!

Since a large part of the inedible carcass is the back, and it is there that one finds a good many small pockets of visible, and hidden, fat, it occurred to Jack that, unless he intended making chicken stock, it might be more reasonable – and less time-consuming – to buy four chicken quarters rather than a whole chicken. So he did. And found that for two pence more, he had the same amount of edible meat, perfect for cooking in his chicken brick with the addition of a little beautifully flavoured liquid.

1½–1¾ hours

Serves 4
    4 chicken quarters
    2 medium-sized onions, chopped
    2 garlic cloves, chopped
    2 celery stalks, chopped
    400 g/14 oz canned tomatoes, drained of half their liquid
    1 tablespoon dry vermouth (optional)
    1½ teaspoons dried oregano
    freshly ground black pepper

Soak the brick in cold water. Remove the skin, and any fat, from the chicken and discard. Drain the brick, wipe off any excess moisture and put the chicken portions inside with the onions, garlic and celery. Put the top on the brick and place in a cold oven. Turn the heat to 180°C/350°F/gas 4 and let the chicken cook for 45 minutes.

Turn the chicken portions over, add the tomatoes and vermouth, if using, then sprinkle over the oregano and pepper to taste. Continue cooking for 45 minutes–1 hour. Serve the chicken with the vegetables and sauce spooned over.

APPLE-BRAISED GUINEA FOWL

Guinea fowl have been domesticated so we can now enjoy these lean, gamebirds all the year round. For this reason I love them, especially in this recipe which keeps them succulently moist.

2–2¼ hours

Serves 6
    2 tablespoons polyunsaturated oil
    3 guinea fowl, giblets and any pockets of fat removed

1 medium-sized onion, chopped
1 garlic clove, finely chopped
4 rashers lean back bacon, trimmed of all fat
3 medium-sized dessert apples, peeled, halved, cored and sliced
2 tablespoons flour
425 ml/¾ pint dry cider
salt (optional) and freshly ground black pepper
350 g/12 oz large mushrooms, wiped with a damp cloth and halved
    through the stems

For garnish
chopped parsley

Heat the oil in a large flameproof casserole over a medium heat. When hot add the birds, 1 or 2 at a time, and brown them well on all sides. Take the pan off the heat, remove the birds and set aside, then heat the oven to 170°C/325°F/gas 3. When the casserole is cool, return it to a low heat and stir in the onion and garlic, cover and cook for 3–4 minutes. Meanwhile, chop the bacon finely, stir into the casserole, cover and continue cooking until the onion is soft but not brown.

Stir the apples into the pan, then sprinkle over the flour. Let the mixture continue cooking, uncovered, until the flour begins to brown. Stir in the cider, season to taste, return the guinea fowl to the pan, add the mushrooms and bring the liquid to the boil. Cover the pan tightly and place in the oven for 1½–1¾ hours or until the meat is tender.

Drain the guinea fowl and transfer them to a cutting board. Cut each bird in half to serve, put the halves on a warmed dish and keep warm. Pour the cooking liquid into a small bowl and spoon off any fat, then pour, with the apples, onions and mushrooms, over the guinea fowl. Garnish with a light sprinkling of parsley and serve.

- Pheasant, when they are in season, are also good in this recipe; use 4 of them.

CRYSTAL-COOKED POUSSIN WITH FIG-MUSTARD SAUCE

This is a simple, but elegant, recipe. So it's a dream for the busy cook-host, or hostess, who also wants to enjoy the party. Or, make half the quantity, and settle down to a good tête-à-tête.

2 hours crystal-cooking the poussins, then 15 minutes

Serves 4
  4 poussins, cleaned
  3 slices fresh root ginger

  For the fig-mustard sauce
  275 ml/½ pint chicken stock
  40 g/1½ oz unsalted butter
  3 tablespoons flour
  2 tablespoons Meaux or similar coarse-grained mustard
  2 tablespoons mild Dijon mustard
  salt (optional) and freshly ground black pepper
  8 canned green figs (about 400 g/14 oz), well rinsed and dried
  about 2 tablespoons dry white wine

Fill a large saucepan, into which the poussins will fit comfortably, with water and bring to the boil. Remove the pan from the heat, add the poussins and ginger, cover, and leave until the water becomes tepid, about 2 hours. That's all there is to it; the meat will be succulent and perfectly cooked.

To make the sauce, first put on the chicken stock to heat, then melt the butter in another saucepan over a medium-low heat and stir in the flour. Cook for 1 minute, stirring, then remove the pan from the heat. Gradually stir in the hot stock and continue stirring until the sauce is smooth. Replace the pan over a medium-low heat and cook, stirring frequently, until the sauce thickens, about 10 minutes. Stir in the mustards, taste and add salt, if wished, and a little freshly ground black pepper. Add the figs and thin the sauce, if necessary, with a little white wine or water, then remove the pan from the heat.

When nearly ready to eat, remove the poussins from the saucepan, draining them well, and take off the skin. Cover the pan and bring the water to the boil, then remove from the heat. Put the poussins back in the water for 1 minute to heat through, then immediately drain them well, and transfer to a warmed serving plate or plates. Reheat the sauce until the figs are warmed through and pour it around the poussins.

- If you want to prepare the sauce in advance, make it without the figs, let it cool, then gently reheat it to serve, thinning with a little hot water and stirring in the figs.

GLAZED POACHED CHICKEN WITH TWO STUFFINGS

'So you've never boned a bird?' Well, I'm here to tell you that with a sharp knife and clear instructions, it is NOT difficult. Nor does it take very long. But oh, the impressive sighs when you serve it, cutting straight through 'the bones' to reveal one or more colourful stuffings. Then you too can say, 'So you've never boned a bird?'

Boning the chicken (about 30 minutes the first time), stuffing and
    poaching it (about 1½ hours), plus cooling and overnight chilling,
    then glazing and chilling (about 1 hour)

Serves 6–8
    1.8 kg/4 lb chicken, cleaned
    salt (optional) and freshly ground black pepper
    about 175 g/6 oz frozen spinach, defrosted and squeezed dry
    2 teaspoons powdered gelatine

For the apricot-walnut stuffing
    1½ tablespoons polyunsaturated oil
    1 medium-sized onion, finely chopped
    125 g/4 oz 'no-soak' dried apricots, finely chopped (otherwise
        soaked for 30 minutes in cold water)
    50 g/2 oz walnuts, chopped
    2 teaspoons chopped, fresh tarragon or ½ teaspoon dried tarragon
    50 g/2 oz dried white breadcrumbs
    salt (optional) and freshly ground black pepper
    1 medium-sized egg white, beaten

For garnish
    fresh tarragon leaves or chives

Bone the bird (see below), then have a drink.
    To make the apricot-walnut stuffing, heat the oil in a small pan over a medium-low heat, add the onion and cook until it softens, stirring occasionally. Transfer to a bowl, stir in the apricots, walnuts, tarragon and breadcrumbs, season to taste, then stir in the egg white.
    Season the inside of the chicken with salt, if wished, and pepper, then stuff with the spinach, spreading it over the bottom. Spread the apricot stuffing over the spinach, pull the two sides of the bird together, and sew them up with a larding needle and heavy thread, using a round

stitch. This will make removing the thread easy. Sew up the neck and tail ends. Transfer the chicken onto the middle of a large oblong piece of muslin. Fold the long sides over the breasts, then tie the ends together. Tie some string round the chicken to secure the muslin.

Choose a flameproof casserole or saucepan large enough to hold the bird, fill it with water and bring to the boil. Lower in the chicken and reduce the heat to gently simmer the water for 40–50 minutes.

Lift the chicken out of the liquid and transfer to a dish to cool. Remove the muslin and string, then refrigerate the chicken overnight. If you have time, add the reserved bones to the cooking liquid and simmer for another 1–2 hours. Cool, then chill the liquid, skimming it of any fat before using as stock.

The next day, sprinkle the gelatine over 275 ml/½ pint hot water and stir briskly until the gelatine has dissolved. Let the gelatine cool until slightly syrupy. I sometimes speed this up by chilling the liquid, but this can be tricky. (If it thickens too much, stir the gelatine over a low heat until it just liquefies, then pour it immediately into a cool container and cool again if necessary.)

Skin the chicken, carefully snipping out the threads, then place the bird, cut side down, on a serving dish. Brush some gelatine over the top of the chicken and chill to set the gelatine. Arrange tarragon leaves or chives in a decorative pattern over the chicken, then brush on another layer of gelatine and chill again. Serve the chicken cold, glistening in aspic.

- Instead of tarragon leaves, you could use flat-leaved parsley – NOT coriander – trimmed well, so that each leaf sits flat, or use the green tops of spring onions, finely shredded (I use a razor blade) and fanned out.

How to bone the chicken

To bone a chicken, turn the bird over onto its breast, then make a slit down its backbone from the neck to the tail end. Remove and discard the parson's nose. Turn the knife at an angle to one side, keeping the edge of the blade against the bone, and cut the flesh away to reveal the carcass down to the leg. Repeat on the other side.

Cut through the sinews between the thighs and legs, then pull out one thigh joint and scrape the flesh away from the thigh bone. Leave the leg bone in place and repeat on the other thigh joint, gently pulling out parts of the carcass as you free the bone. Remove any pockets of fat.

Very carefully cut the ribs away from the flesh, working gradually down to either side of the breastbone, where the flesh and skin are very thin. Cut through the sinews connecting the carcass to the wings, leaving the wings in place, and carefully lift out the ribs and breastbone, cutting against the bones to free any flesh. Put the bones aside to make stock later.

TURKEY STROGANOFF

Fillet of beef is a perfectly good substitute for turkey breast, but I and my purse prefer turkey.

30 minutes

Serves 4
  700–900 g/1½–2 lb boneless turkey breast
  4 tablespoons unsalted butter
  1 medium-sized onion, finely chopped
  225 ml/8 fl oz dry white wine
  450 g/1 lb button mushrooms, wiped with a damp cloth, then thinly
    sliced
  225 g/8 oz plain, Greek-style yoghurt
  ¼ teaspoon tomato purée
  1 teaspoon Dijon mustard
  2 tablespoons freshly squeezed lemon juice
  salt (optional) and freshly ground black pepper

For serving
boiled noodles

For garnish
dill sprigs or freshly chopped parsley

Cut the raw meat in half lengthways, then cut each half across into 6 mm/¼ in strips. Melt the butter in a frying pan over a medium heat and, when hot, add the turkey strips, browning them lightly on both sides, in batches if necessary. Transfer them to a dish and keep warm, then add the onion to the pan, lower the heat and cook until softened but not browned. Meanwhile simmer the wine to reduce by half, then set aside.

Add the mushrooms to the onions and cook for 8–10 minutes or until they release their moisture, stirring occasionally. Raise the heat and stir gently until all the liquid has evaporated. Pour in the wine, add the turkey and bring the wine to a simmer. Cook for about 2 minutes to heat the meat through. Mix the yoghurt in a bowl with the tomato purée, mustard and lemon juice, then turn the heat to low and stir the yoghurt into the pan to heat it through. Season with salt, if wished, and black pepper. Serve the stroganoff with noodles, garnished with dill sprigs or a little chopped parsley.

TURKEY TONNATO

A triumph of flavours, based on the classic Italian dish, *vitello tonnato*, at about one-third of the price. It is ideal for a make-ahead meal, as the turkey breast (thanks to many large supermarkets) and piquant tuna sauce are very simple to prepare, and are served at room temperature.

I always make extra sauce – or make it on its own – to enjoy with pasta, raw or steamed vegetables, grilled or leftover chicken, veal patties. . . .

1¾ hours, plus overnight chilling, then 15 minutes

Serves 6–8
2 × 700–900 g/1½–2 lb boneless turkey breasts, ready for cooking

For the tonnato sauce (makes 225 ml/8 fl oz)
chilled juices of the cooked turkey (see below)
90 g/3½ oz best quality, canned tuna fish in water, drained (use any
    leftover tuna in an omelette [page 75])
1 medium-sized egg white
1 tablespoon capers
1 tablespoon anchovy paste
1 tablespoon freshly squeezed lemon juice
¼ teaspoon cayenne pepper
50 g/2 oz plain, Greek-style yoghurt
salt (optional) and freshly ground black pepper

For garnish
1 tablespoon capers
1 lemon, thinly sliced
small parsley sprigs

Heat the oven to 190°C/375°F/gas 5. If your turkey breast isn't ready in its own foil container, see below; otherwise roast as directed. When cooked, remove the meat from the cooking juices, cool completely, then cover and refrigerate until the meat is cold, or overnight. Pour the juices into a small bowl, cool, cover and refrigerate.

Skim off any fat from the chilled juices and put 1 tablespoon juice into a food processor with the tuna and egg white, then process until smooth. Add the capers, anchovy paste, lemon juice and cayenne pepper, and process until the sauce is smooth. Add the yoghurt and process 2–3 seconds to mix, then taste, add seasoning if wished, and set the sauce aside.

Thinly slice the turkey breasts into 15 mm/½ in wide strips and arrange them, overlapping, on a serving dish. Thin the tuna sauce if necessary by melting the turkey cooking juices over a gentle heat and stirring in just enough to make a coating consistency, then spread evenly over the turkey slices. Garnish with the capers, lemon slices and parsley sprigs and serve.

- You can prepare this dish up to 2 hours ahead by slicing and arranging the meat, then covering the platter with cling film and chilling. Make, cover and chill the sauce, spreading it over the turkey and garnishing just before serving.
- To bone a whole turkey breast, about 2.7 kg/6 lb, lay the meat flat with the breastbone in the centre. With a sharp knife, cut down along one side of the breastbone and continue cutting against the bone as you angle the knife. Gently pull away the meat in one piece from the bone as you cut, to expose the bone. Repeat on the other side. To cook, put the breasts in a foil-lined, butter-greased roasting tin. Thinly spread unsalted butter over the meat, add 2 tablespoons hot water, cover the tin with foil and cook as above for 1½ hours.

GRILLED DUCK WITH BIGARADE SAUCE

Duck has such a wonderful flavour that everyone, especially those of us on low-fat diets, should be able to indulge as often as we wish. Not only have I devised a way to eliminate the fat – of which it has a goodly surplus – and made it easier and faster to cook, but I have also stretched it to feed four, rather than the usual three, from one bird.

The trick is to carve the duck before you cook it. Follow the instructions for cutting the chicken supremes (page 101) but cut through the joints connecting the carcass to the wings. Then cut the thigh-leg joints away from the carcass – and there you are! Your kindly butcher or poulterer may do this operation for you but, *in extremis*, we can do it ourselves.

Once jointed, remove all the fat and skin from the supremes and thigh-leg joints and discard it. Remove as much fat as you can from the carcass and wings, then put them aside to make stock for further economic, and gastronomic, goodies like duck soup (page 19). Cooking will now take much less time than roasting a whole bird as the meat is in small enough portions to grill or poach quickly and easily.

Bigarade is duck's classic, sinfully perfect, complement and the same sauce is very good with chicken, pheasant, pork or any leftovers thereof. The richly flavoured breasts or thigh-leg joints can also be successfully grilled and served with any of the additions given for chicken supremes.

1 hour

Serves 4
    2 duck thigh-leg joints, skin and any fat removed
    polyunsaturated oil, for greasing
    2 boned duck breasts, skin and any fat removed

    For the bigarade sauce
    1 Seville orange, or 1 medium-sized sweet orange and
        1 medium-sized lemon
    4 teaspoons sugar
    3 tablespoons red wine vinegar
    175 ml/6 fl oz espagnole sauce (page 38), defrosted if frozen
    1½ teaspoons cornflour

First prepare the sauce. With a sharp knife, peel away one-third of the Seville orange zest in one piece, or one-third of the sweet orange, and a quarter of the lemon, zest. Carefully slice away any white pith, then cut the zest into very thin batons. Cook in simmering water for 15 minutes, then drain and reserve.

Heat the sugar with 1 tablespoon water in a small heavy saucepan over a medium heat until it just begins to caramelize. Remove the pan from the heat and immediately immerse its bottom in cold water to stop the sugar cooking.

Squeeze the Seville orange or half the sweet orange and a quarter of the lemon and put the juice (about 2 tablespoons) in the saucepan with the caramelized sugar, then add the vinegar. Simmer the mixture to reduce the volume by half. Add the reserved peel, espagnole sauce and about 2 tablespoons hot water to the pan and stir over a low heat. Spoon out a little of the sauce and dissolve the cornflour in it, then stir it back into the sauce and set aside.

Heat the grill to high. When hot, place the thigh-leg joints on a lightly-greased baking tray about 5 cm/2 in under the grill and cook for 2½ minutes each side. This is for rare meat – if you like it better done, cook legs and breasts for another 1–2 minutes. Remove from the grill and keep warm, then grill the breasts for 2 minutes each side. Transfer the meat to warmed serving plates and set aside. Bring the sauce to the boil, stirring, then pour it into a warmed sauceboat. Pour a little of the sauce over the duck joints and serve the rest separately.

- When bitter Seville oranges are in their all too short season, remove about one third of the zest, and cut it into batons as above. Squeeze the oranges, and freeze the juice, with the zest batons, in ice trays. Then you can enjoy this superb dish with the special touch bitter orange gives, cutting more zest batons from a sweet orange if you're very keen.

DUCK IN POMEGRANATE-WALNUT SAUCE

Here is a truly chic dish for you and your nearest-and-dearest. Be warned, however: addiction to the sauce is immediate, so make extra to serve at subsequent meals with other tasty morsels (see below).

1½ hours

Serves 4
    4 boned duck breasts or thigh-leg joints, skin and any fat removed

For the pomegranate-walnut sauce
4 medium-sized fresh pomegranates
juice of 2 lemons, plus extra if needed
1 tablespoon sugar
1 tablespoon polyunsaturated oil
1 medium-sized onion, finely chopped
350 g/12 oz fresh walnuts, chopped
150 ml/¼ pint game stock (page 38)
salt (optional) and freshly ground black pepper

For serving
boiled rice

To make the sauce, scoop the seeds and pulp from the pomegranates into a food processor or blender and process for 20–30 seconds. Strain the liquid into a bowl, stir in the lemon juice and sugar, and reserve.

Heat the oil in a large heavy saucepan over a medium heat. Add the onion and cook, stirring occasionally, until it begins to turn golden. Add the walnuts and stir for 2 minutes. Add the game stock to the pan with the reserved pomegranate mixture and season with salt, if wished, and pepper. Bring the mixture to the boil, stirring occasionally, then reduce the heat and simmer for 20 minutes.

Add the duck breasts and continue to simmer gently for about 20 minutes until the meat is cooked. Meanwhile, prepare some boiled plain, or saffron-flavoured, rice (page 162), preferably using basmati rice.

Put the duck on a warmed serving dish and keep warm. Skim any fat off the sauce with a spoon. Adjust the balance between sweet and sour by adding more lemon juice or sugar to taste. Spoon some of the sauce over the duck and pour the rest into a warmed sauceboat. Serve immediately, accompanied by the rice.

- Pheasant, grouse, guinea fowl, and even chicken breasts are also very fine cooked this way, though duck's slight sweetness lends a perfect balance to the sauce. Just remember that grouse breasts are usually smaller, while the other birds are naturally less moist, so they may cook more quickly than the duck.
- I always freeze extra sauce, then reheat it gently to serve with grilled duck, chicken or other poultry, grilled or fried minced beef patties (pages 126–8), or minced veal or pork patties.
- Prepare extra pomegranate juice to freeze in ice cube trays, then transfer the cubes to a freezer bag. You can then make this dish any time of the year, and add some of the juice to fruit salads (page 179).

MEAT

STEAK TARTARE

BEEF PATTIES WITH RED WINE-ROSEMARY SAUCE
Peppercorn and whisky sauce
Mushroom, cream and cognac or brandy sauce

HERBED MEAT LOAF
Italian meat loaf
Goulash loaf

VEAL-SAGE PATTIES IN YOGHURT-MARSALA SAUCE
Green peppercorn patties
Chilli-jam sauce

HEAVENLY GOULASH

PORK STEAKS 'GIN AND BEETHOVEN'
Pork steaks with peppercorn sauce

LAMB AND CASHEW STEW

BRAISED GAMMON WITH MADEIRA SAUCE

BRAISED VEAL AND TOMATOES

SPICY LAMB PATTIES

CASSOULET JACK SPRAT

LAPIN MARIE-PIERRE

BRAISED FRANKFURTER BEEF
BRAISED SHOULDER OF LAMB
Sorrel/spinach stuffing
Rice and chervil stuffing
BEEF STROGANOFF (*see Poultry*)

I grew up eating beef in Texas, where sheep and lamb were dirty words, and veal was a financial loss for an industry that makes money from fattening cattle for prime, marbled steaks. Sounds gruesome . . . Even so, beef remains an occasional pleasure for me, as do pork, veal and even lamb, usually when having friends to dinner.

To stay on any diet there has to be some enjoyment, and if that takes the form of an occasional piece of meat, well, *bon appetit*! Meat does have more than its fair share of saturated fat, but this can be largely avoided by choosing the leaner, unmarbled cuts and trimming off any visible fat, preferably before cooking. The small amount of fat that remains in the meat itself is largely unsaturated.

When we prepare and cook it ourselves, we know how lean the meat is. This isn't usually the case when we order it away from home. For instance, lean beef mince contains 10 per cent fat, but the average beefburger you buy has nearly 30 per cent! The recipes which follow endeavour to make an occasional excess less wickedly indulgent, but still temptingly delicious.

STEAK TARTARE

An occasional treat I enjoy tremendously is steak tartare. Because the meat is raw and minced, it is very tender, highly nutritious, and extremely delicious with all its highly flavoured additions. Many people prefer not to eat raw meat, while others pass it by because to be good the tartare must be made from the most expensive, prime cuts – fillet or sirloin. These are fairly lean but there are other cuts of beef as lean, or leaner, often better tasting and almost as tender. Besides, once minced, even tough meat will be relatively tender.

I have tried making steak tartare with lean, minced leg tops (also known as 'leg of mutton cut' from the foreshoulder of the beef), sirloin and with fillet. And I have found that minced fillet on its own actually lacks flavour, while leg top lacks elegance. Minced sirloin and rump are both excellent, the sirloin being marginally better – and much more expensive. When comparing the four minced cuts, alone, and in various combinations with friends, all agreed that the best mince in flavour, and price, was a combination of rump and leg tops.

With a food processor, it's easy to repeat the trial yourself. (Your butcher won't want to mince less than about 1.4 kg/3 lb of meat, because it would get lost in his big mincer.) Buy about 125 g/4 oz of each cut of meat, trim away any visible fat – weighing it to calculate how much you've paid for it – then chop the meat into pieces. Put each variety separately into a food processor, fitted with the metal blade, and process for 5 seconds, then taste the different cuts of minced beef individually and in various combinations. Mix any leftovers into one delicious patty, or enjoy your trial with a friend or two.

Now, when I buy mince I select 2 lean cuts of beef, leg tops for flavour and rump for tenderness. My obliging butcher removes any visible fat, then minces the meats together in his machine – three times for superior texture. The result is lean, tender and delicious – suitable for grilling, frying, and even steak tartare. It is also much easier on the pocket than buying minced fillet, sirloin or rump on its own. Any not used immediately is divided into individual portions and frozen.

10 minutes

Serves 2–4
    125 g/4 oz beef leg tops, all visible fat removed
    125 g/4 oz rump or sirloin steak, all visible fat removed
    1 spring onion, finely chopped
    1 tablespoon small capers, chopped

1 tablespoon chopped fresh dill, or 2 teaspoons finely chopped
   parsley
1 large egg yolk
Tabasco sauce
salt and freshly ground black pepper

For garnish
1–2 spring onion tops, finely chopped
1–2 teaspoons whole capers
1 tablespoon chopped fresh dill, or 2 teaspoons finely chopped
   parsley

Cut the meat into large dice, mix the two types together and put them in
a food processor. Process for 5–6 seconds only, then transfer the meat to
a bowl.

Add the spring onion, the chopped capers, the dill or parsley and the
egg yolk to the meat. Season with 2–4 drops Tabasco sauce, salt and
freshly ground pepper to taste, then mix well.

Form the steak tartare into one large patty, or smaller individual
patties, place on a serving plate or plates, and garnish the meat by
surrounding it with sections of finely chopped spring onion, whole
small capers and chopped dill or parsley.

If not serving the steak tartare right away, cover it with cling film to
keep the meat bright red and refrigerate for up to 2 hours.

BEEF PATTIES WITH RED WINE-ROSEMARY SAUCE

Any prime beef cut as a steak, with or without bone, can be cooked in
this fashion, but for tenderness and flavour, I prefer a mixture of
super-lean leg tops and rump, minced professionally. I buy enough of
the mixture to make at least 8 × 175 g/6 oz patties, some of which I
wrap individually in cling film and freeze together in a plastic bag.

If necessary, I defrost them overnight or during the day in the
refrigerator. Then it's an easy matter to prepare a quick, delicious
mixed salad or a steamed vegetable with lemon juice and pepper
sprinkled over, before pan-frying the meat. What makes this combination a gourmet treat, of which I and my friends never seem to tire, is the
quick and easy sauces poured over the meat, a few of which are given
below.

10 minutes

Serves 1
 1 tablespoon polyunsaturated oil
 150–175 g/4–6 oz minced lean beef steak, formed into a patty about
    25 mm/1 in thick, defrosted if frozen
 4–6 tablespoons dry red wine
 1 small rosemary sprig, or ½ teaspoon dried rosemary
 1 tablespoon (or ½ cube) espagnole sauce (page 38), or 2–3
    teaspoons unsalted butter
 salt (optional) and freshly ground black pepper

For serving
 mixed salad or steamed vegetable (optional)

If serving a salad, vegetable or any other accompaniment, prepare it
first, then put aside.

Heat the oil in a small frying pan over a medium-high heat, swirl it
around the pan and add the meat. For rare meat with a crispy brown
exterior, cook the patty for 3 minutes, then turn and cook for a further
2–3 minutes. For medium meat, reduce the heat slightly a few seconds
after adding the patty to the hot oil and cook for 8–9 minutes, turning
once. Remove the pan from the heat and transfer the meat to a serving
plate.

Replace the pan over a medium-low heat and add the wine. Bruise
but do not grind the rosemary in a pestle and mortar and add it to the
wine with the espagnole sauce or butter. Season with salt, if wished, and
pepper. When the sauce has reduced to 1–1½ tablespoons, pour it over
the meat and serve with the salad or vegetables – and the rest of the
bottle of wine.

- For peppercorn and whisky sauce, mix together ½ teaspoon each of black
  and white peppercorns, allspice berries and freeze-dried pink and green
  peppercorns, or pink and green peppercorns in brine, drained. Add them
  to the pan over a low heat with 2–3 tablespoons whisky and 1 tablespoon
  (or ½ cube) espagnole sauce or 2–3 teaspoons butter. When reduced to
  1–1½ tablespoons, pour it over the meat and serve.
- For mushroom, 'cream' and cognac or brandy sauce, heat 1 tablespoon
  polyunsaturated oil with 2 teaspoons butter over a medium-low heat, then
  add 2–3 very finely sliced or chopped button mushrooms, stirring
  continually for 1 minute or until they soften. Turn the heat to low,
  sprinkle over 1–2 teaspoons cognac or brandy, then immediately add 3
  tablespoons plain, Greek-style yoghurt and stir continually until the
  sauce reduces to 1–1½ tablespoons. Pour over the meat and serve.
- On the same principle, try creating your own combinations such as
  chopped spring onions and walnuts with whisky and espagnole sauce or

butter; brandy, a tiny touch of tomato purée, and a little good chilli powder; oil and butter with a canned, drained and sliced artichoke heart, white wine, pepper and yoghurt, etc.
- Do try the patties grilled or pan-fried and served with pomegranate-walnut sauce (pages 120–1).
- All the sauces above will be good with grilled or pan-fried veal escalopes and chops, and pork steaks or chops.

HERBED MEAT LOAF

Another excellent way of using my lean, well-flavoured mince is to mix in chopped herbs and other tasty additions, then bake the mixture as a loaf. This is a more relaxed way of cooking for several people than grilling, and any leftover meat loaf makes a perfect sandwich filling.

40–50 minutes

Serves 4–6
   900 g/2 lb lean minced beef
   2 tablespoons chopped green tops of spring onions, or fresh herbs
      such as chives, green garlic, sage or marjoram, or 1 tablespoon
      dried herbs
   salt (optional) and freshly ground black pepper
   1 medium-sized egg white

Heat the oven to 180°C/350°F/gas 4. Work the meat, the spring onion greens or herbs, salt, if using, and pepper together well with your hands. Add the egg white, mixing it thoroughly into the meat, then form into a loaf. Put it into a 900 g/2 lb loaf tin and bake for 30–35 minutes for rare meat and 40–45 minutes for medium meat.

- Alternative recommended additions include 2 tablespoons Roquefort sauce (pages 95–6) instead of the egg white; chopped fresh lovage or celery leaves; chopped walnuts; finely chopped field mushrooms.
- 'Italian meat loaf' could well become one of your most popular main courses – as it is mine – when you add 1 tablespoon bruised fennel seeds, 1 tablespoon dried oregano, 2–3 tablespoons freshly grated Parmesan cheese, freshly ground black pepper and 1 medium-sized egg white to 900 g/2 lb of good mince and bake as above. If you fancy ½–1 teaspoon chopped green chilli – seeded if wished – then add that, too.
- Goulash loaf is such a favourite that I always make extra goulash (page 130) and freeze it in small quantities in order to turn highly respectable meat loaf into a gourmet's – low-fat or otherwise – heaven.

Mix 225 g/8 oz lean minced beef and 225 g/8 oz cold goulash together with your hands. Work in an egg white and bake as above. Serve with remoulade sauce (page 41), low-fat soured cream with chopped chives, or, better still, with savoury-sweet chilli sauce!

- To stretch your meat loaf deliciously but economically, work in 50 g/2 oz low-fat croûtons (page 175), pulverized with a rolling pin.

VEAL-SAGE PATTIES IN YOGHURT-MARSALA SAUCE

Veal patties make a nice change in the daily fare, though I can continue to enjoy them with different sauces for days.

25 minutes

Serves 4
700 g/1½ lb lean veal, all fat removed, then diced
25 g/1 oz parsley, stems discarded
1 small onion, finely chopped
2 medium-sized eggs
2–3 teaspoons chopped fresh sage or 1–1½ teaspoons dried sage
4 tablespoons flour
2–3 tablespoons polyunsaturated oil
4 tablespoons dry marsala
125 g/4 oz plain, Greek-style yoghurt mixed with 1 tablespoon
    freshly squeezed lemon juice
freshly ground black pepper

Briefly process the first five ingredients in a food processor. The mixture should be rather coarse. Form the veal mixture into four patties and dust them lightly with flour.

Heat the oil in a frying-pan over a medium-low heat. When it is hot, carefully lower the patties into the pan and cook them for 4 minutes or until well browned on one side. Turn, and cook the other side.

Transfer the patties to a hot serving dish and keep warm. Add the marsala to the pan over a low heat, scraping up any bits left in the pan with a spoon. Stir in the yoghurt and cook for 1–2 minutes, stirring occasionally. Pour the sauce over the meat and serve.

- For another delicious treat try the above with ½ teaspoon drained green peppercorns or freeze-dried green peppercorns instead of the sage, but

serve the patties and sauce with thinly sliced rounds of seeded yellow pepper.
- Try the patties, too, with sage, served with a sauce of the yoghurt stirred with 1 tablespoon chilli jam (page 41).

HEAVENLY GOULASH

The secret of this dish is to use the finest quality paprika, preferably Hungarian. I always make this recipe in large quantities – to freeze, and to flavour other meat dishes (page 128).

2½–3 hours

Serves 6–8
    1.4 kg/3 lb leg tops or other cut of lean beef
    2–3 tablespoons polyunsaturated oil
    700 g/1½ lb onions, chopped
    3 tablespoons paprika
    4–6 tablespoons red wine vinegar
    1 tablespoon caraway seeds, ground in a pestle and mortar
    1½ teaspoons juniper berries, crushed
    1½ tablespoons marjoram leaves, or 1½ teaspoons dried marjoram
    1 large potato, finely diced
    salt (optional) and freshly ground black pepper

For serving
    1–2 tablespoons finely chopped lovage leaves (optional)

Cut the meat into small bite-sized pieces, removing all visible fat and gristle, then set aside.

Heat 2 tablespoons of oil in a large, flameproof casserole or heavy-based saucepan over a medium-low heat. When hot, add the onions, cover and leave them to sweat, very gently, for about 30 minutes or until they are very soft, stirring occasionally. (Check after 15 minutes and add more oil only if necessary.) Heat the oven to 180°C/350°F/gas 4.

Stir in the paprika and vinegar, then the caraway seeds, juniper berries and marjoram. Lastly stir in the meat and potato and transfer the mixture, if necessary, to a casserole. If the lid does not fit tightly, be sure to cover the casserole with foil before putting on the lid. Cook for 1½–2 hours, stirring occasionally. The finished stew will thicken as the meat and potato begin to disintegrate. Season with salt, if wished, and pepper. Stir in the lovage leaves, if using, just before serving.

PORK STEAKS 'GIN AND BEETHOVEN'

Another firm favourite with my friends, this dish was musically – or alcoholically? – inspired. One day, a few years ago, my father was listening to a newly-acquired set of Beethoven symphonies. I arrived home during Symphony No. 5, shattered after a lesson in conversational Arabic, and joined him in a pitcher of gimlets. During the Eighth Symphony, he asked me what was for dinner? I wasn't sure what ingredients were in the kitchen, or if the cook could stand up to get there. But by the opening bars of the Ninth, we were enjoying this.

about 10 minutes

Serves 2
   2 tablespoons olive oil
   2 × 225 g/8 oz pork steaks, cut to an even thickness and trimmed of
      all fat
   1½ teaspoons coriander seeds
   2–3 tablespoons Meaux, or similar coarse-grained, mustard
   ½ teaspoon ground ginger
   freshly ground black pepper
   4 tablespoons plain, Greek-style yoghurt
   ½–1 teaspoon freshly squeezed lemon juice

Heat half the oil in a small frying pan over a medium-low heat. When hot, add the pork and cook for about 4 minutes each side or until done. Meanwhile, crush the coriander seeds in a pestle and mortar and stir them into the mustard with the ginger, the rest of the oil and black pepper to taste.
   When the pork is cooked, transfer it to warmed serving plates, turn the heat to low and stir the mustard mixture around the pan for about 1 minute, scraping up any sediment in the pan. Stir in the yoghurt and lemon juice, immediately remove the pan from the heat and pour the sauce over the meat: a 'Song – or mouthful – of Joy'.

   • For another treat, try grilled or pan-fried pork steaks with peppercorn
     sauce (page 127).

LAMB AND CASHEW STEW

Ismail Merchant is one of the most charming people, let alone cooks, I've ever had the pleasure of eating with or cooking for. He said I could share this brilliant recipe with you. It's low-fat, of course.

1¼–1½ hours

Serves 5–6
     6 tablespoons polyunsaturated oil
     900 g/2 lb boneless lean lamb, cut into large, bite-sized pieces
     8 medium-sized onions, chopped
     ½ tablespoon salt
     8 cloves
     8 peppercorns
     3 cinnamon sticks
     1 tablespoon caraway seeds
     1 tablespoon cumin seeds
     4–5 bay leaves
     225 g/8 oz plain, Greek-style yoghurt
     8–10 garlic cloves, chopped
     3 tablespoons coriander leaves, finely chopped

     For the chilli paste
     125 g/4 oz canned green chillies, drained, or 3–4 fresh green chillies, seeded
     6 mm/¼ in fresh ginger root
     6 garlic cloves

     For the cashew paste
     100 g/4 oz cashews
     3 tablespoons sesame seeds
     3 tablespoons poppy seeds

     For serving
     mixed green salad

Heat 4 tablespoons oil in a large saucepan over a high heat. When hot add the lamb and cook, stirring frequently, until it is browned on all sides, about 5 minutes. Remove the lamb from the pan with a slotted spoon and reserve. Turn the heat to medium, add another tablespoon of oil and the onions then cook, stirring frequently, until the onions soften, 7–8 minutes.

Return the lamb to the pan with the salt, spices, bay leaves and hot water to cover. Bring to the boil, then simmer for 25 minutes or until the meat is cooked but not tender. Drain off and reserve the water, skimming off any fat.

Meanwhile, make the chilli paste by processing the chillies, ginger root and garlic to a paste in a food processor, or in batches in a blender, and reserve. For the cashew paste, purée the nuts and seeds similarly, and reserve. Add the chilli paste to the lamb and gently simmer the mixture over a low heat for 10–15 minutes, adding a few tablespoonfuls of the reserved stock as necessary to prevent burning. Add the cashew paste and simmer for another 10–15 minutes, adding stock as necessary. Add the yoghurt and let it simmer for 5 minutes, then pour in some more stock, according to the thickness of sauce you desire. Simmer gently until the meat is tender, adding a little more stock if necessary.

Heat the last tablespoon of oil in a small saucepan over a medium-low heat and add the garlic. When it is golden, add to the stew with the chopped coriander, cover immediately and cook gently for a further 5 minutes. Uncover just before serving, and accompany with a mixed tossed salad.

BRAISED GAMMON WITH MADEIRA SAUCE

Since it will earn maximum applause for minimum exertion, here is another excellent candidate to serve at a dinner party. It will remind your friends how lucky they are to know you, impress your in-laws or celebrate the arrival (or departure) of a loved one – and leave you a glorious stock to make soup for yourself.

2¼ hours cooking the meat, then 10 minutes

Serves 8–10
   1.4–1.8 kg/3–4 lb boneless middle gammon in one piece, any visible
      fat removed
   4 medium-sized carrots, sliced
   1 large onion, studded with 8–10 cloves
   1 sprig fresh, or ¼ teaspoon dried, thyme
   2 bay leaves, crumbled
   4 parsley sprigs
   5 black peppercorns
   275 ml/½ pint dry white wine

For the sauce
400 ml/14 fl oz espagnole sauce (page 38), defrosted if frozen
3 tablespoons Madeira

Calculate the cooking time for the meat based on 65 minutes per kg/30 minutes per lb, plus 30 minutes. Put the meat into a heavy flameproof casserole, cover with cold water and bring slowly to the boil. Drain the meat and discard the water.

Return the meat to the casserole with the carrots, the onion, thyme, bay leaves, parsley sprigs and peppercorns. Pour in the wine and 275 ml/½ pint water and bring to the boil. Reduce the heat to very low, cover and cook for about 1½ hours or until the meat looks pink and opaque, and feels firm. Top up with a little extra water, if necessary, during the cooking. Remove the pan from the heat and let the meat cool in its cooking liquid.

When ready to eat, bring the cooking liquid to the boil, then gently simmer the meat for about 10 minutes to reheat it. Drain the meat and place on a warm serving dish. Save the stock for soup.

Just before serving, bring the espagnole sauce to the boil and cook for 1 minute. Remove the sauce from the heat, stir in the Madeira and pour into a warmed sauceboat. Carve the ham at the table and serve with the sauce handed round separately.

BRAISED VEAL AND TOMATOES

Comforting and quite delicious, I do recommend this dish. It – and you – will become everyone's favourite.

3¼–3¾ hours

Serves 6
    1.4 kg/3 lb boneless shoulder of veal
    2 tablespoons flour
    6 tablespoons olive or other polyunsaturated oil
    2 medium-sized onions, chopped
    2 garlic cloves, chopped
    200 ml/7 fl oz chicken stock (page 37)
    150 ml/¼ pint dry white wine
    1 tablespoon tomato purée
    2 sprigs fresh, or ½ teaspoon dried, thyme

½ teaspoon dried savory (or use 3 sprigs fresh, or ¾ teaspoon dried, thyme)

½ teaspoon salt (optional) and freshly ground black pepper

450 g/1 lb tomatoes, blanched, skinned, seeded and chopped, or 275 g/10 oz canned tomatoes, drained and seeded

1 large pepper, seeded and chopped

225 g/8 oz button mushrooms, wiped with a damp cloth, and halved

50 g/2 oz black olives, stoned, if wished, and wiped free of any oil if necessary

Cut the veal into 5 cm/2 in dice, removing any fat or gristle. Coat the meat lightly and evenly with flour, shaking off the excess and set it aside. Heat 4 tablespoons oil in a frying pan over a medium-high heat; when hot, add the veal and brown it quickly on all sides, in batches if necessary. Transfer the meat to a flameproof casserole.

Heat the oven to 180°C/350°F/gas 4. Pour off all but 1 tablespoon of the oil in the frying pan, replace the pan over a low heat, add the onion and garlic and cook for 5 minutes, stirring occasionally. Pour in the stock and wine, then add the tomato purée, herbs, salt, if wished and a little freshly ground black pepper. Bring to the boil, then simmer for 1½ minutes, stirring occasionally. Stir in the tomatoes and pepper, then pour the mixture over the meat in the casserole. Bring the liquid again to a simmer, cover tightly, using a layer of foil under the lid if necessary, and place the casserole in the oven for 2–2½ hours or until the meat is very tender.

Just before serving, heat the remaining 2 tablespoons of oil in a small pan over a medium-low heat. When hot, add in the mushrooms and olives and cook for about 5 minutes, stirring occasionally. Mix the mushrooms and olives into the veal and tomatoes, and serve immediately, from the casserole.

SPICY LAMB PATTIES

cooking the potatoes, then 20–25 minutes

Serves 6

1.2 kg/2¾ lb lean, boneless lamb, all visible fat removed, then cut into large dice

4 cm/1½ in fresh ginger root, peeled and cut into 3–4 pieces

2 large potatoes, boiled until tender, then peeled and chopped

1 green chilli, seeded and chopped (optional)
125 g/4 oz plain, Greek-style yoghurt
½ teaspoon salt
1 teaspoon coarsely ground black pepper
1 tablespoon polyunsaturated oil, for greasing

Heat the grill to high. Put the lamb, with the ginger, potatoes, chilli (if using), yoghurt, salt and pepper in a food processor. Process for about 30 seconds or until the mixture is a coarse purée.

Form into 6–8 patties, about 7.5 cm/3 in in diameter, and place them flat on a greased roasting pan.

Place the pan 20–22.5 cm/4–5 in under the grill and cook for 12–15 minutes, turning once, for medium meat, or longer if wished. Serve immediately.

CASSOULET JACK SPRAT

At least once a year, usually in cold weather, I make cassoulet, an awesomely delicious casserole traditionally 'floating' in goose fat, lard, salt pork and fatty sausages. Mine has about one-third of that fat and, what little it might lose in flavour, it compensates for in digestibility – and fewer calories.

As making cassoulet is quite a production, consider doubling the quantities as I do and freezing the unused portion in individual, ovenproof containers, sprinkling over extra breadcrumbs to cover each little cassoulet well. Once topped, and wrapped with heavy foil, and frozen, you and yours can easily enjoy cassoulet more than once a year.

8–12 hours soaking, then 5 hours

Serves 8–10
800 g/1¾ lb haricot beans
100 ml/4 fl oz polyunsaturated oil
800 g/1¾ lb goose or duck joints, all skin and visible fat removed
6 medium-sized onions, chopped
6 garlic cloves, crushed
125 g/4 oz tomato purée
400 g/14 oz canned tomatoes
2 teaspoons paprika
1½ teaspoons cayenne pepper
salt (optional)

2 bouquets garnis
500 g/18 oz lean pork shoulder, cut into 25 mm/1 in cubes
6 shallots or 2 small onions, chopped
25 g/1 oz flour
700 ml/1¼ pints light beef stock
freshly ground black pepper
2 cinnamon sticks
1 large onion, stuck with 6 cloves
1 large carrot
2 whole heads of garlic, unpeeled, plus 1 extra garlic clove, peeled
    but left whole
1 pork or beef shin bone (optional)
500 g/18 oz gammon in 1 piece
200 g/7 oz garlic sausage, in 1 piece
6–8 'country-style' sausages (75–80% pork meat content)
125 g/4 oz dried fresh breadcrumbs

Pick over and wash the beans, then soak them, covered in plenty of cold water, overnight.

Heat the oil in a large, heavy-based saucepan over a medium heat, add the goose or duck joints and fry until they are golden, about 5 minutes. Remove the joints and reserve them, then pour off three-quarters of the oil and reserve that too. Add the chopped onions and crushed garlic to the pan and stir for 2–3 minutes over a medium heat. Stir in the tomato purée, add the canned tomatoes, paprika, cayenne, salt and 1 bouquet garni. Return the goose or duck pieces to the pan, cover and cook over a very low heat for 2½–2¾ hours. Add a little water, if necessary, from time to time, to prevent burning.

In another heavy pan, heat 2 tablespoons of the reserved oil and lightly fry the cubes of fresh pork. When evenly coloured, add the chopped shallots or onions, sprinkle on the flour, stir for 1–2 minutes and then gradually add half the stock, still stirring. Season with salt and pepper, add the cinnamon sticks, cover tightly and simmer, extremely gently, for 2–2½ hours.

Drain the beans, put them in a large saucepan, cover well with fresh cold water, add the onion stuck with cloves, the carrot, garlic heads, shin bone (if using), gammon and the second bouquet garni. Bring to the boil and simmer for 1½ hours. Season the beans with salt, if wished, add the garlic sausage and simmer a further 20 minutes.

Remove the 2 pans containing the meats from the heat, uncover, check the seasoning (which should be rather strong). Reserve. Remove the gammon and garlic sausage from the bean saucepan and set them aside to cool slightly. Drain the beans and discard the onion, carrot, shin bone, garlic heads and bouquet garni. Cut the gammon into 25 mm/1 in dice. With a slotted spoon, remove the duck and pork pieces from their respective sauces and set aside. Discard the bouquet garni and the cinnamon sticks, and combine both sauces with the drained beans and the rest of the stock.

Rub a large earthenware or cast iron casserole with the remaining garlic clove, then spoon a generous layer of the bean mixture into the dish. Lay 2 or 3 pieces of duck or goose on top of the beans, then some of the pork and gammon cubes and 3 or 4 thick slices garlic sausage. Cover with another layer of beans and repeat the process, finishing with a layer of beans. Heat the oven to 230°C/450°F/gas 8.

Put the remaining reserved oil into a frying pan and fry the country sausages until they are three-quarters done. Tuck the sausages into the top layer of beans, and sprinkle with fat from the frying pan and the breadcrumbs. Put the dish near the top of the oven for about 20 minutes or until the top is nicely browned and the whole dish well heated through. Serve from the casserole at the table.

LAPIN MARIE-PIERRE

Rabbit is wonderful meat and needs some good press! Not only is it practically nil in fat, it's cheap, so go and buy some bunny and try this recipe, which was first cooked for me a few years ago by a dear friend.

about 1 hour

Serves 6
    4 tablespoons polyunsaturated oil
    6 leg joints of rabbit (about 700 g/1½ lb)
    4 medium-sized onions, chopped
    2 teaspoons powdered English mustard
    225 ml/8 fl oz dry white wine
    3–4 sprigs fresh thyme, or 1 teaspoon dried thyme
    1½ tablespoons tarragon-flavoured, or other French aromatic
        mustard
    3 tablespoons plain, Greek-style yoghurt

For garnish
chopped fresh herbs (thyme, tarragon, chives, mint etc.), or
  chopped parsley

Heat the oven to 100°C/200°F/gas low. Put the oil in a flameproof casserole over a medium-high heat. When hot, brown the rabbit joints quickly on both sides, in batches, then put them aside. Lower the heat, add the onions, and cook, stirring frequently until they begin to brown.

Return the rabbit to the casserole with the powdered mustard, wine and thyme. Bring the wine to the boil, cover and place in the oven for 35–40 minutes. Do not overcook, or the rabbit will toughen and Marie-Pierre and I will be in your bad books.

To finish, remove the casserole from the oven and transfer the rabbit to a serving dish. Stir the herb mustard into the wine-onion sauce, add the yoghurt, then pour the sauce over the rabbit portions. Sprinkle with one or more chopped herbs, or parsley, and serve.

- Don't be tempted to overdo the mustard, as too much can make the dish taste soapy.

BRAISED FRANKFURTER BEEF

Here is a treasure. The recipe was given to me by Hans and Gretel Beer, in whose home I first enjoyed the dish. This low-fat version of it will become a party-piece for you, too.

about 2½ hours

Serves 6
  1.1–1.4 kg/2½–3 lb joint of lean beef, such as leg-of-mutton cut
  6 all-meat (pork) frankfurter sausages
  salt (optional) and freshly ground black pepper
  1½ tablespoons polyunsaturated oil
  1 large onion, chopped
  about 1 tablespoon flour
  2 teaspoons paprika
  125 g/4 oz plain, Greek-style yoghurt, or low-fat soured cream (page 42)
  2 tablespoons lemon juice

Make 6 evenly spaced holes through the joint, with the grain of the meat, using a larding needle. Widen the holes as necessary with the handle of a wooden spoon and push the sausages through the holes. Cut off the ends of the sausages, chop and reserve them. Rub the meat all over with salt, if wished, and plenty of freshly ground black pepper.

Heat the oven to 170°C/325°F/gas 3. Heat the oil in a frying pan over a medium-high heat. When hot, add the meat and brown it on all sides. Reduce the heat to medium-low and transfer the meat to a casserole. Add the chopped onion and cook until the onion begins to brown, stirring occasionally. Sprinkle over the flour, stir for about 1 minute, then add the onion to the casserole.

Add 275 ml/½ pint water to the frying pan and stir with a metal spoon or spatula to scrape up any tasty bits and pour this over the meat. Add the paprika and the reserved pieces of the sausages. Cover and put the casserole in the oven for about 2 hours or until the meat is tender, adding a little hot water during cooking if necessary.

Transfer the meat to a hot dish and keep warm. Put the braising liquid (with all the solids) into a food processor or blender and coarsely purée, then strain through a sieve into a small saucepan, pressing hard to extract all the juices. Cook, quickly, until the liquid begins to boil, then remove the pan from the heat. Mix the yoghurt and lemon juice together, then stir into the sauce and pour into a sauceboat.

Slice the meat so that each piece has rounds of sausage in it. Serve with the sauce handed round separately.

- The sauce for this dish is so incredibly good that I always add 1–2 extra chopped frankfurters to the casserole, and sometimes a little extra yoghurt or hot water to the braising mixture. If my guests aren't too greedy, enough will be left to reheat gently, to accompany any leftovers or to add flavour to another dish the next day.

BRAISED SHOULDER OF LAMB

Inexpensive and easy, this is a low-fat twist on traditional English fare, yet it retains the very best of springtime flavours – at any season of the year.

about 1 hour

Serves 6
1.6 kg/3½ lb lean shoulder of lamb, boned
1 large onion, chopped
4 large garlic cloves, chopped
1 small green or red pepper, chopped
salt (optional) and freshly ground black pepper
rosemary
150 ml/¼ pint dry white wine

For serving
new potatoes (optional)

Use a sharp knife, or ask the butcher to remove as much visible fat as possible from the boned cavity of the lamb shoulder, leaving the thin layer of back fat on the outside of the meat, then roll and skewer the meat as necessary to secure it. Tie round the roll with kitchen string, several times at intervals, and once or twice lengthways to make a neat, tight roll. Remove the skewers, if wished. Heat the oven to 180°C/ 350°F/gas 4.

Put a flameproof casserole or heavy saucepan over a medium-high heat and when hot, quickly sear the meat on all sides. Remove the meat, lower the heat to medium, add the onion and garlic and stir with a wooden spoon. They will quickly soften. Remove the pan from the heat.

Add the meat to the pan with the chopped pepper, salt if using, pepper, rosemary and wine. The liquid should be about 25 mm/1 in in depth, so add a little water if necessary. Heat until just boiling, cover the pan and place in the oven for 25 minutes for medium-rare meat, 30 minutes for medium, or 35 for medium-well done meat.

If wished, add new potatoes, cooked until just tender, to the meat, 5 minutes before serving.

- A special touch to enhance the glory of this dish is to stuff the meat before rolling. Fresh sorrel and/or spinach gives a beautiful flavour. Use 225 g/ 8 oz fresh, trimmed leaves. Blanch them, refresh in cold water and squeeze dry, then finely chop and spread over the meat.
- Another excellent stuffing is made by mixing 125 g/4 oz cooked rice (40 g/1½ oz uncooked) with 2 tablespoons chopped fresh chervil, or 2 teaspoons dried chervil.

VEGETABLES AND PULSES

BUTTER BEANS IN TOMATO-PINEAPPLE SAUCE
Pinto beans in tomato-pineapple sauce

FÈVES AU VIN

CRÊPES BOMBAY

TOMATO MUNG BEANS

CLOVE-LEMON LENTILS

CHICK PEA AND CHICKEN PALETTE

FRESH CORN OFF THE COB

CARROT PURÉE 'VICHY'

STEAMED COURGETTES WITH GINGER

FRENCH BEANS WITH COURGETTE SAUCE

VEGETABLE FLORETS EN PAPILLOTE

BRAISED CHICORY
Braised celery
Braised turnips

STEAMED POTATOES AND ARTICHOKES

STEAMED POTATOES AND ONIONS WITH LOW-FAT MAYONNAISE
With low-fat soured cream
With courgette sauce

BAKED POTATOES WITH SAGE AND WALNUTS
Baked sweet potatoes with sage and walnuts

STEAMED CAULIFLOWER WITH ANISE AND DILL

STEAMED FENNEL WITH PEPPER RINGS AND MINT

FROZEN GREEN PEAS COOKED TO TASTE LIKE FRESH ONES (see *Eggs*)

SPICED DAL (see *Eggs*)

Vegetables are celebrities in my kitchen. They have no fat, and no cholesterol (unless you smother them in butter). Steaming is the best way to cook them as it preserves vitamins, minerals and much of their colour, texture and taste – everything a low-fatty could want. Too often are vegetables just an afterthought ('meat and two veg'), served heaped on a plate in a miserable jumble. In France and the East, vegetables are accorded their rightful place as a course on their own. Perfect seasonings for them are plain yoghurt, lovely fresh herbs and freshly squeezed lemon or lime juice, which is tangy but not as sharp as lemon.

Pulses – peas, beans and lentils – are a mainstay for me. As for soup, there is an almost endless variety of pulse dishes, from warm and hearty to puréed and refined, all of them good sources of nutrition (and fibre). Once I worried if I didn't eat poultry, meat or cheese every day. Now my conscience, purse and palate are reassured when I tuck into a bowl of lentils with a dollop of yoghurt.

We are very lucky in the variety of dried, Indian pulses available from many grocers, and more and more supermarkets. They add enormously to our potential for devising and enjoying new dishes. A thoughtful Indian grocer also kindly introduced me to the ground spice, asafoetida. A small amount added to the simmering pulses is a quick alternative to draining after the first boiling, then reboiling in fresh water until tender. Both methods aid digestion and help prevent flatulence.

Do remember that all dried pulses should be picked over to remove any stones, seeds or straw, and most have to be soaked in plenty of cold water before being cooked. Lentils are the exception, as are the hulled and split Indian pulses usually called 'dal'. Soaking is best done overnight, though except for chick peas and sometimes brown lentils, it isn't absolutely necessary. If you have forgotten to soak them the previous night, place the pulses in a saucepan, cover them with plenty of cold water and bring it to the boil. Let the water boil for about five minutes, remove from the heat, cover and leave for about 2 hours.

Drain all soaked pulses and cook them in fresh water, boiling them, particularly kidney beans, very vigorously for at least ten minutes to destroy any toxicity. Cooking times vary, depending on how the pulses were dried and how old – i.e. tough – they are. The greater their age, the longer cooking time will they need. Since this is an unknown quantity, always allow for extra time, checking after the minimum recommended, then cooking for longer if necessary.

BUTTER BEANS IN TOMATO-PINEAPPLE SAUCE

A dish of butter, or pinto, beans in a tart tomato sauce sweetened with pineapple is just the thing to wake up a tired palate and improve life. Serve it with raisin corn bread for a real feast!

overnight soaking, then about 3 hours

Serves 4
    450 g/1 lb butter or pinto beans, picked over
    3 medium-sized onions, halved lengthways, then cut and divided
        into halfmoon slices
    175 g/6 oz tomato purée
    175–225 g/6–8 oz canned crushed pineapple or pineapple chunks,
        drained
    3–4 teaspoons cider or white wine vinegar, or lemon juice
    about 2 teaspoons runny honey (optional)
    Tabasco sauce (optional)
    salt (optional) and freshly ground black pepper

For serving
boiled rice (page 161) or raisin corn bread (page 174)

For garnish
fresh mint sprigs (optional)

Soak the beans for 8–12 hours, or overnight, in plenty of water to cover. Drain the beans, put them in a saucepan and cover with fresh water. Bring to the boil, reduce the heat, then simmer for about 2½ hours, occasionally adding extra hot water to keep the beans covered.

Drain and rinse the beans in hot water, then put them back in the pan with the onions. Process the tomato purée and 350 ml/12 fl oz water with the pineapple in a food processor, or blender. Add vinegar, adjusting the amount to taste, to the tomato sauce and a little honey, if wished, to balance the tartness. Pour the mixture into the saucepan, bring to the boil, reduce the heat and simmer until the beans are tender, about 30 minutes. Taste and add Tabasco sauce and seasoning, if wished. Serve on a bed of boiled rice, garnished with fresh mint sprigs if available.

FÈVES AU VIN

A pot of beans simmering in the kitchen definitely improves my day, especially when at the end of it there will be this elegant, if simple, little dish to enjoy with a glass of wine, a loaf of bread and good company.

overnight soaking, then about 3 hours

Serves 4
    450 g/1 lb pinto or borlotti beans, picked over
    225 g/8 oz lean bacon or gammon, trimmed of all fat and finely
        diced
    3 medium-sized onions, chopped
    2 garlic cloves, chopped (optional)
    2 bay leaves, crumbled
    2 sprigs fresh thyme, or 1 teaspoon dried thyme
    1 bottle (700 ml/1¼ pint) respectable dry red wine
    225 g/8 oz button mushrooms, wiped with a damp cloth
    salt (optional) and freshly ground black pepper

    For serving
    crusty bread
    mixed salad

Soak the beans for 8–12 hours, or overnight, in plenty of water to cover. Drain, put them in a saucepan and cover well with fresh water. Bring to the boil, reduce the heat and simmer for 2½ hours, topping up with more hot water as necessary.

Drain the beans and rinse in hot water, drain again, then return to the pan with the bacon, onions, garlic if using, bay leaves and thyme. Pour in all but about 150 ml/¼ pint of the wine and add hot water to the pan, if necessary, to cover the beans. Reserve the rest of the wine and bring the mixture to the boil, then reduce the heat so the wine simmers gently until the beans are tender, from 30 minutes.

Cut the mushrooms into quarters or, if they are large, into smaller pieces, and stir them into the beans. Cook for about 5 minutes, season to taste, stir in the rest of the wine and serve with crusty bread and a mixed salad.

CRÊPES BOMBAY

This is easily one of the most beautiful and exquisitely flavoured dishes you could ever make. The lovely black and white pulses, *urid dal*, are available at Asian grocers and many supermarkets.

about 2½ hours

Serves 4–6
225 g/8 oz urid dal, picked over
850 ml/1½ pints chicken stock (page 37), warmed to simmering point
4 bay leaves, crumbled
2 green chillies

For the coriander crêpes (makes 12)
125 g/4 oz flour
3 medium-sized eggs
225 ml/8 fl oz milk
1 bunch fresh coriander, stalks discarded
melted butter for greasing
225–350 g/8–12 oz cooked ham, fat discarded and finely diced

For the chilli-saffron sauce
40 g/1½ oz unsalted butter
3 tablespoons flour
275 ml/½ pint skimmed milk, warmed to simmering point
6–8 saffron strands
salt (optional)

For serving
crisp tossed mixed salad

Put the pulses in a saucepan and wash them in cold running water until the water is quite clear. Drain, then fill the pan with plenty of fresh water to cover the pulses. Bring to the boil, reduce the heat and simmer for 20 minutes.

Meanwhile, make the crêpe batter. Whisk the flour and eggs together in a bowl, then whisk in the milk. Add the coriander leaves to the batter, and leave it for 2 hours to thicken. If necessary, beat in a very little water, just before cooking, to return the batter to the consistency of thin cream.

Drain and rinse the pulses in a colander and return them to the pan. Add the hot chicken stock, or a mixture of chicken stock and hot water, and the bay leaves. With the tip of a sharp knife, cut 5–6 slits lengthways over (but not right through) the surface of the whole chillies and add them to the pan.

Bring the liquid to the boil, reduce the heat and simmer gently for 1½ hours or until the pulses are tender but remain separate, stirring occasionally. Drain in a colander and leave to cool, stirring occasionally. Discard the bay leaves and reserve the chillies.

Meanwhile, cook the crêpes. Dip a piece of absorbent paper in melted butter and rub lightly around a 20 cm/8 in frying or crêpe pan over a medium-low heat. When hot, stir the crêpe batter and add about 3 tablespoons to the pan, tilting the pan to cover the bottom with batter. Cook for about 1 minute or until the crêpe becomes dry on top.

Using a flexible metal spatula, lift up the crêpe gently and flip it over on its other side and cook for about 30 seconds. Transfer to a plate and cover it with a piece of greaseproof paper to prevent the crêpes from sticking together. Rub the pan with more melted butter and cook the rest of the crêpes.

To make the sauce, melt the butter in a saucepan over a low heat, then stir in the flour and cook for 1 minute, stirring frequently. Remove the pan from the heat and stir in the hot milk and saffron. Continue stirring until the sauce is smooth, then return the pan to a low heat, stirring continually until the sauce thickens, 3–4 minutes. Remove the pan from the heat and season with salt, if wished.

Heat the oven to 180°C/350°F/gas 4. Seed the chillies, if wished, and slice them across thinly. Stir the chillies into the sauce and reserve.

Stir the diced ham into the pulses and put 3–4 tablespoons of the mixture in a line along one side of each crêpe, then roll up. Transfer the crêpes, seam-side down, to a large foil-lined baking tin and spoon half the sauce over the crêpes. Cover the pan with foil and bake for 10–15 minutes to heat them through.

Using a spatula, transfer the crêpes to serving plates. Thin the remaining sauce with a little milk, stirring over a low heat, then pour over the crêpes. Serve immediately with a crisp tossed mixed salad and dry white wine.

TOMATO MUNG BEANS

The white beansprouts so familiar in Chinese cookery are sprouted from mung beans. Here the beans themselves are used in a very tasty dish, excellent served with grilled or roasted meat and poultry.

2 hours soaking, then about 2½ hours

Serves 6
    450 g/1 lb mung beans, picked over
    1½ tablespoons polyunsaturated oil
    1 medium-sized onion, chopped
    1 teaspoon cumin seeds
    2 bay leaves, crumbled
    3 medium-sized tomatoes
    425 ml/¾ pint chicken stock (page 37)
    1 teaspoon salt
    1–2 chillies, seeded and finely chopped

Wash the beans and soak them in plenty of water for 2 hours, then drain well. Heat the oil in a saucepan over a medium-low heat. When hot, add the onion, cumin and bay leaves and cook, stirring occasionally, until the onion begins to brown.

Add the drained beans, tomatoes, stock, salt, chillies and 150 ml/¼ pint hot water. Bring to the boil, then simmer the mixture over a very low heat for 1½–2 hours until the pulses are tender, adding more hot water if necessary. Transfer to a hot serving dish and serve immediately.

CLOVE-LEMON LENTILS

Trading one's birthright for a dish of lentils may not be advisable, but you can happily sup on these with slices of brown bread, yoghurt and a salad. They can also become an exciting accompaniment to meat or poultry (see below).

30–40 minutes

Serves 4–6
- 2 tablespoons polyunsaturated oil
- 1 medium-sized onion, chopped
- ½ teaspoon cloves
- 225 g/8 oz whole green lentils, picked over
- 400 ml/14 fl oz canned beef consommé
- ⅛ teaspoon asafoetida (optional)
- juice of 1–1½ lemons
- freshly ground black pepper
- plain, Greek-style yoghurt (optional)

Heat the oil in a saucepan over a medium-low heat. When hot, add the onion and cook, stirring occasionally until it begins to brown, about 5 minutes. Add the cloves and lentils and cook for 5 minutes, stirring occasionally.

Add the consommé, 425 ml/¾ pint hot water and the asafoetida, bring to the boil, then simmer very gently for 20–30 minutes or until the lentils are tender. Stir in the lemon juice and plenty of freshly ground black pepper. Serve the lentils hot with a dollop of plain thick yoghurt on each serving, if wished.

- Purée the hot, drained lentils in a food processor or blender to make a very delicious accompaniment to grilled meat or poultry.

CHICK PEA AND CHICKEN PALETTE

This beautiful dish is suitable for an elegant lunch or smart supper. And you can cook it well ahead of time, then dress the plates an hour or so before serving.

overnight soaking, then 3¼ hours plus cooling

Serves 6
- 225 g/8 oz yellow chick peas, picked over
- 225 g/8 oz brown chick peas, picked over (see below)
- 2 cinnamon sticks
- 4 bay leaves, crumbled
- 6 chicken breasts, wings removed
- salt
- 125 ml/4 fl oz olive oil

50 g/2 oz pine nuts
large bunch fresh marjoram, or flat-leaved parsley
freshly ground black pepper
6 medium-sized firm, ripe tomatoes
juice of 1–2 lemons

Wash the yellow and brown chick peas separately, then cover, each in a separate bowl, with plenty of fresh water and soak for 8 hours or overnight.

Drain and rinse the yellow chick peas, put them in a small saucepan and cover with hot water. Add 1 of the cinnamon sticks and 2 of the bay leaves and bring to the boil. Repeat with the brown chick peas. Simmer the pulses gently for 2½–3 hours or until they are tender but not soft.

Drain the cooking liquid from the yellow chick peas and refresh under cold running water to stop them cooking. Drain through a colander, then put aside, discarding the cinnamon stick and bay leaves. Repeat with the brown chick peas. Once the pulses have cooled, you can refrigerate them to serve the next day.

While the chick peas are cooking, or the next day, add the chicken breasts to a large saucepan of boiling salted water. As soon as the water comes back to a simmer, reduce the heat and simmer for 10–12 minutes or until the meat is just cooked. Immediately remove the breasts from the liquid and let them cool.

Heat the olive oil and pine nuts in a saucepan over a low heat, stirring frequently for about 5 minutes, or until they start turning deeply golden. Immediately remove the pan from the heat, and stir in the marjoram or parsley, ¼–½ teaspoon salt and plenty of freshly ground black pepper. Add to the yellow chick peas, mixing well in.

Skin the chicken breasts and pull the meat off the bones. Slice each breast across thinly, keeping the slices together to retain the original shape. Core the tomatoes, then slice thinly into rings. Reshape each tomato.

One hour before serving, spread a portion each of the yellow and brown chick peas, in 2 thick lines down the middle of a dinner plate. Squeeze lemon juice generously over the brown chick peas. Next to the yellow chick peas, arrange one of the chicken breasts, overlapping the slices slightly. Then spread down one of the sliced tomatoes, next to the brown chick peas. Repeat for the 5 other dinner plates.

• Brown chick peas are a darker version of yellow chick peas. Both types are sold by Asian grocers and many supermarkets.

FRESH CORN OFF THE COB

When I was an innocent, fat kid, hot corn on the cob dripping with butter was a summertime favourite. This dish is better.

30 minutes

Serves 4–6
4–6 corn on the cob
1 tablespoon canned, drained chopped pimiento (optional)
about 1 tablespoon freshly squeezed lime juice
125–175 g/4–6 oz plain, Greek-style yoghurt, at room temperature
freshly ground black pepper

Stand each corn cob on its end and remove the kernels from the cob, cutting down with a sharp knife. Put the kernels in a steamer over bubbling water, cover and cook for about 10 minutes. The kernels will be cooked but should still be crunchy.

Stir the kernels, pimiento, if using, and lime juice into the yoghurt. Season generously with pepper, add more juice if wished and serve.

- Freshly squeezed lemon juice is a good substitute in this dish when limes aren't available.

CARROT PURÉE 'VICHY'

Try this low-fat twist on carrots Vichy the next time you serve lamb, pork or chicken or just feel like something warm, comforting and 'carrot'.

about 1 hour

Serves 4–6
900 g/2 lb carrots
25 g/1 oz butter
1 teaspoon sugar
salt (optional) and freshly ground pepper
freshly grated nutmeg

Scrub the carrots and peel them if necessary, then put them into a large heavy saucepan with the butter and just cover with water. Cook over a medium heat for 45 minutes, topping up with water as necessary.

When they are tender, raise the heat slightly and reduce the water to about 125 ml/4 fl oz. Drain and reserve the water for soup. Purée the carrots in a food processor or blender until they are very smooth, then season the mixture with salt, if wished, pepper and freshly grated nutmeg. Serve the purée warm.

STEAMED COURGETTES WITH GINGER

With grilled meat and poultry, this is a great dish for people who like courgettes, and for people who think they don't like courgettes.

10 minutes

Serves 4
    350–450 g/12 oz–1 lb smallish courgettes
    2–3 teaspoons grated fresh ginger root
    lemon juice

Top and tail the courgettes, then cut into rounds about 6 mm/¼ in thick. Put them into the top of a steamer, or on a collapsible steamer inside a saucepan over water. Scatter over the ginger, cover and bring the water to a simmer, then steam for 5–6 minutes, or until the courgettes are tender but not soft.

Transfer the courgettes to a serving dish, squeeze over lemon juice to taste and serve immediately.

FRENCH BEANS WITH COURGETTE SAUCE

A simple creation that will make your guests gasp with pleasure and surprise. It is also sensible for a dinner party as you can cook the vegetables ahead, then steam briefly to reheat.

about 10 minutes

Serves 4
450 g/1 lb French beans
3 medium-sized courgettes
3–4 tablespoons plain, Greek-style yoghurt
salt (optional) and freshly ground black pepper

Top and tail the beans and put them into the top of a vegetable steamer or a collapsible steamer inside a saucepan over water. Cover and bring to a simmer and cook until the beans barely begin to soften – anything from 2 to 4 minutes depending on their size.

Meanwhile, top and tail the courgettes and cut them into rounds about 20 mm/¾ in thick. When the beans are ready, add them to the steamer and continue cooking another 2–4 minutes or until the beans and the courgettes are just tender.

Leaving a few courgette rounds with the beans to keep warm, transfer the rest to a food processor or blender and purée with 1 tablespoon of the yoghurt. Stir in the rest of the yoghurt and serve immediately over the beans and remaining courgettes.

- If not serving immediately, refresh the vegetables under cold running water, drain and reserve. Steam briefly to reheat and continue with the recipe.

VEGETABLE FLORETS EN PAPILLOTE

about 30 minutes

Serves 4
1 small cauliflower
450 g/1 lb broccoli
175 g/6 oz button mushrooms, wiped clean
freshly ground black pepper
2 tablespoons lemon juice
25–40 g/1–1½ oz butter, cut into small pieces

Heat the oven to 180°C/350°F/gas 4. Cut the cauliflower and broccoli into small florets and save the stalks for soup. Cut the mushrooms into quarters through their stems, trimming the ends if necessary.

Cut two pieces of foil, each about 28 cm/11 in square. Divide the florets and mushrooms along the centre of each sheet, grind over some pepper, sprinkle on the lemon juice, then dot with the butter.

Fold the foil over the vegetables, into a rectangle or triangle, then fold the edges together twice to seal tightly and put the parcels on a baking tray in the oven for 20–25 minutes. Serve immediately from the parcels, giving each person some of the lovely juices.

BRAISED CHICORY OR CELERY

People know you care about cooking, and about them, when you take the little extra trouble to serve a braised vegetable. Its melting texture provides a thoughtful contrast to a second vegetable served crisp and steamed, or crunchy and raw.

30–40 minutes

Serves 4
    4 heads of chicory or 1 large celery heart
    425–575 ml/¾–1 pint chicken stock (page 37)
    15 g/½ oz unsalted butter (optional)

Put the vegetables into a small heavy-based saucepan or flameproof casserole, trimming them to just fit. Pour in the stock to come three-quarters of the way up the vegetables, bring to the boil, reduce the heat to low and cover tightly. Cook for 20–30 minutes, or until the chicory or celery is tender. Transfer to a serving dish and keep warm. Reduce the stock over a high heat to about 150 ml/¼ pint, add the butter if wished and pour over the vegetables. Serve very hot.

- Braised turnips are a favourite variation of mine on the above recipe. Peel 450 g/1 lb small turnips, steam for 10 minutes, then put in a saucepan with 50 ml/2 fl oz espagnole sauce (pages 38–9) and an equal amount of water. Cover and place over a low heat for 4–5 minutes, shaking the pan occasionally. Superb with grilled or pan-fried beef patties.

STEAMED POTATOES AND ARTICHOKES

When big appetites are coming to a special dinner party, this simple and lovely dish is a good one to include on the menu.

15 minutes

Serves 4–6
    450 g/1 lb potatoes, scrubbed
    200 g/7 oz canned artichoke hearts, drained and sliced
    2 tablespoons canned, drained pimientos, cut into thin strips
        (optional)
    coarsely ground black pepper
    75–125 g/3–4 oz low-fat mayonnaise (page 43)

Cut the potatoes into 15 mm/½ in thick slices and put into the top of a steamer, or a collapsible steamer inside a saucepan over water. Cover, bring the water to a simmer and steam for 10 minutes or until the potatoes are just tender. Add the sliced artichokes to the steamer, cover and remove the pan from the heat.

When ready to serve, stir the hot or warm potatoes and artichoke hearts together with the pimientos, if using, freshly ground black pepper and low-fat mayonnaise. Serve at once.

STEAMED POTATOES AND ONIONS WITH LOW-FAT MAYONNAISE

Here is one of the most satisfying dishes I know and filling enough to make a whole meal with a lovely salad.

10–15 minutes

Serves 4
    4 medium-sized to large potatoes, scrubbed
    1–2 onions, sliced and divided into rings
    1–2 tablespoons chopped dill, parsley or tarragon, or ½ teaspoon
        dried herbs
    125–225 g/4–8 oz low-fat mayonnaise (page 43) or plain, Greek-style
        yoghurt

Cut the potatoes into 15 mm/½ in thick slices. Put them with the onion rings into the top of a steamer over water. Cover, bring to a simmer and steam for 10 minutes or until the potatoes are tender. Serve hot, sprinkling with herbs, if wished, and spooning the mayonnaise or yoghurt on top.

- Low-fat soured cream (pages 42–3) and a grating of nutmeg also make steamed potatoes and onions a very special dish.
- Courgette sauce (page 154) is another scrumptious addition to steamed potatoes and onions!

BAKED POTATOES WITH SAGE AND WALNUTS

Soft and piping hot, baked potatoes make a lovely meal or accompaniment when they are sliced open and piled high with chopped herbs and other low-fat fillings. Depending on what's available, mine include mixtures of green garlic, tarragon, chives, mint, marjoram and dill, thin yoghurt, low-fat Roquefort dressing (pages 95–6), soured cream (pages 42–3) or a sprinkling of herb vinegar and, always, plenty of freshly ground black pepper.

baking the potatoes, then 5 minutes

Serves 1
   1 baked potato
   ¼ fresh lemon (optional)
   25 g/1 oz chopped walnuts
   about 6 sage leaves, chopped
   1–2 heaped tablespoons plain, Greek-style yoghurt
   coarsely ground black pepper

Hold the potato in a tea cloth, rub and squeeze it slightly to break up the inside. Cut a cross in the top and squeeze in the lemon juice, if wished. Scatter over the walnuts and sage, top with yoghurt, grind over the pepper and serve.

- The same filling is particularly good with baked sweet potatoes.

STEAMED CAULIFLOWER WITH ANISE AND DILL

15 minutes

Serves 4–6
   1 medium-sized cauliflower
   1½ teaspoons aniseed, bruised in a pestle and mortar
   1 teaspoon chopped fresh dill or ½ teaspoon dried dill weed
   juice of 1 large lemon

Cut the cauliflower into florets. If the stems are thick, cut a cross in the bottoms to speed cooking. Put the florets into the top of a steamer, or into a collapsible steamer inside a saucepan over water. Cover, bring the water to a simmer and steam for 8 minutes or until the cauliflower is tender but not soft.

Transfer to a warmed serving dish, sprinkle over the aniseed and dill, then squeeze over the lemon juice. It's best to serve this immediately, though you can keep the dish covered while putting the finishing touches to the rest of the meal.

STEAMED FENNEL WITH PEPPER RINGS AND MINT

10 minutes

Serves 4
   4 small bulbs of fennel
   1 small green or red pepper, seeded and sliced into thin rings
   small handful of fresh mint leaves
   lemon juice

Cut off the stems, and any green feathery sprigs from the tops of the fennel, and reserve the sprigs for a salad. Trim the bottom of the bulbs, if necessary, and cut them lengthways, from top to bottom, into slices about 6 mm/¼ in thick.

Place the fennel in the top of a steamer, or in a collapsible steamer inside a saucepan over water. Cover, bring the water to a simmer and steam for 5–6 minutes, or until the fennel is tender yet still slightly firm. Transfer to a serving dish, scatter over the pepper rings and mint leaves, then squeeze over lemon juice to taste. Serve immediately.

RICE, PASTA, PIZZA
AND BREAD

BOILED LONG-GRAIN, WHITE AND BROWN RICE

BASMATI RICE

Saffron rice

Herbed rice

RICE PILAV

Mushroom pilav

VEGETABLE RISOTTO

CLAM AND PARMESAN PASTA

GIARDINARA SAUCE

TOMATO SAUCE

MACARONI AND CHEESE

VERMICELLI ALLA SALSA CRUDA

GARLIC, PEPPER AND WALNUT PASTA

NOODLES WITH BASIL SAUCE, PINE NUTS AND MANGO

LOW-FAT PIZZAS

CORN BREAD WITH RUM-SOAKED RAISINS

Rum-soaked raisins

LOW-FAT CROÛTONS

More pleasurable to me than potatoes is rice, which makes frequent appearances at my table – on its own with a little good stock, as an accompaniment to a main course, or as a main dish in tandem with a salad, or pulses. Pasta, too, *without* buttery, creamy sauces, is another boon to low-fat eating. It is inexpensive, available in a huge variety of shapes, many of which I always keep on hand in the larder for a change in the daily menu. And, most importantly, for unexpected meals with unexpected guests. Fresh pasta is even better than dried, and easily made at home with a machine – easier still to buy – and it cooks in about a quarter the time.

Homemade pizza is fun and deserves many plaudits. Make it in quantity and freeze in individual pizza portions. While it thaws, dream up the fanciful toppings that can be made from the low-fat ingredients to hand. Some of my favourites are given for your pleasure, and to inspire you in devising your own.

Good baked bread recipes are given in many other books, but I do share a recipe for the type I'm most partial to, corn bread. The corn bread I knew from childhood was wonderfully flavoured but tended to be dry. This never mattered because we stuffed hot chunks with butter, letting it melt and ooze. My corn bread is moist, needing no butter – only a taste to make it one of your favourites, too.

BOILED RICE

There are many kinds of rice and even more ways of cooking it. People's preferences are also varied. Some souls like it soft, with the grains gummy, others expect the grains to be separate and chewy without being gritty. Since different kinds of rice cook differently, the only solution is to use a basic recipe, then find the variety you like the best, and learn the amount of time, and liquid, necessary to give you a pleasing result.

Long-grain brown, or Thai, rice is my favourite, though I'll happily eat well-cooked white rice, especially if it has chopped herbs, a little good stock, or a well-flavoured sauce with it. Instant, or minute, rice is an abomination, but quite heavenly is the nutty-flavoured white rice known as basmati.

Long-grain white or brown rice

about 25 minutes

Serves 4
    225 g/8 oz long-grain white or brown rice
    ⅛–¼ teaspoon salt

Measure the rice in a cup, then put aside. Measure twice the amount – or volume – of water and bring it to the boil in a small saucepan. Immediately add the rice and salt, bring back to the boil and boil for 30 seconds. Cover the pan and turn the heat very, very low. Cook for 20 minutes.

If the rice is then tender and wet, continue cooking without the lid until the excess water evaporates. If the rice is still too firm, and there is still water in the pan, cover and continue cooking for another 5 minutes. If, on the other hand, your rice is too firm and dry, add 4 tablespoons boiling water, cover and cook for a further 5 minutes.

Once you know the correct timing for your preferred variety of rice, you'll be able to cook it without having to adjust the time – or volume of liquid needed.

- Long-grain white or brown rice is also delicious in saffron and herbed rice variations (page 162).

BASMATI RICE

30 minutes soaking, then 20 minutes

Serves 4
    225 g/8 oz basmati rice
    ⅛–¼ teaspoon salt

Measure the rice and note its volume. Pick it over and remove any small stones, then put in a large bowl. Wash the rice in several changes of gently running cold water until the cloudiness (caused by excess starch) is gone and the water quite clear.

Soak the rice in fresh cold water for 30 minutes, then drain well and put into a small saucepan with one and one-third times its measured volume of water. Add the salt. Bring to the boil, then cover tightly and turn the heat very low. Cook for 15 minutes or until the rice grains are tender.

- Saffron rice with its pale golden colour and seductive fragrance is easy to make and impressive to serve, especially with leftovers. To make it, remove 1–2 tablespoons of water from the amount you need to cook the rice. Soak 2–4 saffron strands in 1–2 tablespoons hot water for 10 minutes, then add the water and saffron to the pan when you cook the rice.
- For herbed rice take a handful of mixed, chopped, fresh herbs and stir into the rice just before serving.

RICE PILAV

Pilavs – a mixture of rice and vegetables, or meat, poultry or fish, are deliciously simple, substantial – and nutritious. Here is my basic recipe – the variations are endless, and up to you.

25 minutes

Serves 4
    25 g/1 oz butter
    2 tablespoons polyunsaturated oil
    1 medium-sized onion, chopped
    225 g/8 oz long-grain, brown or white rice
    425 ml/¾ pint chicken stock (page 37)

salt (optional) and freshly ground black pepper
finely chopped parsley or other fresh herbs

Heat the butter and oil in a saucepan over a medium-low heat, add the onion and cook for 5 minutes or until the onion softens. Stir in the rice and cook for 1 minute, then add the chicken stock and bring to the boil. Lower the heat, cover, and simmer gently for about 15 minutes or until the rice is tender and has absorbed all the stock.

Taste, add salt, if wished, and pepper, then fork in the parsley or herbs. Serve right away, or cover the pan and keep the pilav warm until ready to serve.

- For mushroom pilav, soak 15 g/½ oz dried ceps or *porcini*, or 3 dried Chinese mushrooms, in a little warm water for 20 minutes. Reserve the soaking liquid and thinly slice the ceps or *porcini*, or discard the stems from Chinese mushrooms and thinly slice the caps. Coarsely chop 125 g/4 oz button mushrooms.

  Measure the reserved soaking water and add enough chicken stock to make up 425 ml/¾ pint liquid. Add the dried and fresh mushrooms to the pilav when the stock comes to the boil and continue cooking as above.

VEGETABLE RISOTTO

Good risottos demand more attention than some other dishes, but a labour of love never tasted so good. They also demand *arborio*, or Italian, rice as it absorbs more liquid than long-grain rice to give a creamier end result.

about 45 minutes

Serves 6
   1.9 litres/3¼ pints chicken stock, hot (page 37)
   2 tablespoons polyunsaturated oil
   25 g/1 oz butter
   1 large onion, finely chopped
   400 g/14 oz arborio or other medium-grain rice
   2 celery stalks, finely chopped
   1 medium-sized carrot, finely diced
   175 g/6 oz tender French beans, cut into 15 mm/½ in pieces
   175 g/6 oz shelled fresh peas, or frozen peas, defrosted

2 medium-sized tomatoes, blanched, peeled, seeds and juice
  removed, the flesh diced
3 small courgettes, diced
50 g/2 oz freshly grated Parmesan cheese
salt (optional) and freshly ground black pepper

Bring the stock to the boil, then cover and keep it warm over a low heat.

Heat the oil and butter in a heavy-based saucepan over a low heat, add the onion and cook until transparent. Add the rice to the pan and stir for about 1 minute to coat the grains with the fat. Add about 275 ml/½ pint of the hot stock and stir continually with a wooden spoon until the stock has been absorbed. Add another 150–225 ml/5–8 fl oz of the hot stock and again stir constantly until it, too, has been absorbed.

After 10 minutes' cooking – and gentle stirring – add the celery, carrot, beans and fresh (but not frozen) peas and continue stirring, adding more hot stock when all the liquid has been absorbed. Continue stirring in the stock, a little at a time, for 10 minutes, then add the defrosted frozen peas, tomatoes and courgettes. Continue to cook, stirring and adding more stock as necessary.

When, after about 30 minutes, all the stock has been absorbed, take the pan off the heat. Stir in the Parmesan, taste, add salt, if wished, and pepper. Cover the pan so the cheese melts and combines with the rice. Serve immediately.

- If you know your risotto must wait before being enjoyed, under-cook it by about 5 minutes. Just before serving, finish cooking it with a little more stock, then add the cheese and seasoning, and serve at once.

CLAM AND PARMESAN PASTA

With this simple recipe, a small jar of clams and some dried pasta in the larder will be a welcome sight at the end of a long day – or when hungry friends arrive unexpectedly.

15 minutes

Serves 4
5 tablespoons olive oil
1 tablespoon salt (optional)
350 g/12 oz dried tagliatelle or spaghetti
1 small onion, finely chopped

125 g/4 oz tiny clams in brine, drained, rinsed and dried well on
    absorbent paper
1 tiny garlic clove, chopped (optional)
4 tablespoons freshly grated Parmesan cheese

Bring a large saucepan of water to the boil, add 1 tablespoon oil and salt,
if wished, then the pasta. Cook for 10 minutes or until the pasta is
tender yet firm to the bite, then drain immediately.

Meanwhile, heat 3 tablespoons oil in a small saucepan over a low heat.
Add the chopped onion and cook until softened but not coloured, about
3 minutes.

Add the clams and garlic, if wished, and stir briskly for 30 seconds.
Stir in half the cheese and the rest of the oil and cook for about 1 minute.
Remove from the heat and cover to keep warm. To serve, reheat the
clams briefly, then toss into the drained pasta with the rest of the cheese.

GIARDINARA SAUCE

A beautiful low-fat sauce that lives up to its name with a taste 'fresh
from the garden'. Serve it with pasta, or even with baked potatoes,
steamed courgettes, fish or poultry.

30 minutes

Serves 6
    2 medium-sized carrots, scraped
    2 medium-sized courgettes
    3 tablespoons olive oil
    1 small onion, finely chopped
    4 bacon rashers (about 125 g/4 oz), fat removed, diced
    1 teaspoon fennel seeds, bruised in a pestle and mortar
    400 g/14 oz canned tomatoes
    225 g/8 oz fresh broccoli
    225 g/8 oz button mushrooms, wiped with a damp cloth, and sliced
    salt and freshly ground black pepper,
    2 tablespoons chopped parsley
    2 tablespoons finely grated Romano or Parmesan cheese

Cut the stem ends off the carrots and slice them in half lengthways.
Divide each piece again in half lengthways then slice across into

5 cm/2 in lengths. Slice each section lengthways into thin batons. Repeat with the courgettes and reserve the 2 vegetables separately.

Heat the oil in a small saucepan over a low heat. Add the onion, diced bacon, and fennel seeds, then cook until the onion is soft but not coloured, about 3 minutes. Stir in the carrot batons and tomatoes, with their juice, cover and cook for 10 minutes, stirring occasionally.

Meanwhile, trim the tender florets from the broccoli and discard the rest. Separate the florets into individual pieces. When ready, stir them into the carrots, cover and cook for 5 minutes, stirring occasionally.

Add the courgette batons and mushrooms, season to taste, cover and cook for a further 5 minutes, stirring occasionally. Remove from the heat and uncover. To serve, reheat briefly if necessary, stir in the parsley and mix the sauce into hot pasta with the cheese.

TOMATO SAUCE

Homemade tomato sauce is usually used with pasta or pizza, but do yourself, and your loved ones, a favour and try spooning it over cooked vegetables, chicken, fish or pork.

25 minutes

Makes about 225 ml/8 fl oz
    900 g/2 lb firm ripe tomatoes, or 2 × 400 ml/14 oz canned tomatoes,
        drained
    30 ml/2 fl oz olive oil
    ½ teaspoon sugar
    1 small garlic clove, chopped (optional)
    salt (optional)

Halve the fresh tomatoes and squeeze or spoon out all the seeds. Put the tomato halves or the drained, canned tomatoes in a saucepan with the oil, sugar and garlic, if wished. Cook over a very low heat for 6–7 minutes, stirring frequently.

Transfer the mixture to a sieve and let it drain over a bowl for 10 minutes, then discard the liquid. Press the tomatoes through the sieve, then taste and add salt if wished. Use immediately, or refrigerate for up to 4 days.

- When you see how good this little sauce is, be tempted, next time you make it, into adding a tiny chopped chilli, a strip of orange zest, a chopped fresh sage leaf, a small piece of cinnamon stick, or other flavouring to complement the dish the sauce is to accompany.

MACARONI AND CHEESE

Be misled: I want you to try this recipe. It is as simple and straightforward as the traditional dish of the same name. But my version has a wonderfully savoury flavour with only about one-tenth of the fat. And, since the dish contains practically no cheese, it is easier on the purse – as well as the waistline!

45 minutes–1 hour

Serves 4
   350 g/12 oz dried macaroni or similar pasta
   1 tablespoon polyunsaturated oil
   40 g/1½ oz unsalted butter
   3 tablespoons flour
   575 ml/1 pint skimmed milk
   1 tablespoon Marigold Swiss vegetable bouillon, or other powdered
      vegetable stock
   freshly ground black pepper
   Parmesan cheese, preferably freshly grated

Bring a large saucepan, about three-quarters full, of water to the boil. Pour in the macaroni and add the oil to prevent the pan foaming over with starch, and the pasta from sticking together. Boil for about 10 minutes until just tender. Drain the macaroni through a sieve and set aside.

    Meanwhile, heat the oven to 180°C/250°F/gas 4. Melt the butter in a saucepan over a medium-low heat, add the flour and stir with a wooden spoon for about 1 minute, reducing the heat if necessary to prevent burning. Remove the pan from the heat. Heat the milk with the powdered vegetable stock in another saucepan until almost boiling, then pour it gradually into the butter and flour (alias the roux), stirring with the wooden spoon or a hand whisk until the sauce is smooth. Replace the saucepan over a medium-low heat and cook, stirring frequently, for about 5 minutes or until the sauce begins to thicken.

Stir the macaroni into the sauce, then into a 1.1 litre/2 pint soufflé, or other ovenproof, dish or individual dishes. Grind over and stir in pepper to taste, then grate over Parmesan cheese, again to taste. Bake, uncovered, for 40 minutes – 25 minutes in individual dishes – or until the top begins to brown, though not so long that the mixture dries out. Serve very hot.

- In less traditional moments I often stir goodies like 1 tablespoon chopped pimiento, or chopped walnuts, or 1 teaspoon chopped fresh chillies into the mixture before topping with the Parmesan and baking.
- As this dish freezes well, it's a good idea to make extra and freeze in small, or individual, freezer and ovenproof containers. For impromptu meals it can be cooked from frozen, making it the perfect standby.

VERMICELLI ALLA SALSA CRUDA

Superlatives are not enough for this dish. Its flavour, and appearance, is utterly exquisite, while the simplicity and timing of preparation makes it perfect even for a dinner party. Try it out on yourself and another loved one; the experience will be memorable.

15–20 minutes

Serves 4
    50 g/2 oz tender fresh, French beans, topped and tailed
    25 g/1 oz small, tightly closed, button mushrooms, wiped with a
        damp cloth
    25 g/1 oz Mozzarella cheese
    8 leaves fresh basil
    8–10 sprigs fresh parsley
    ½ garlic clove
    1 very small tomato, blanched, skinned and halved, all seeds and
        liquid discarded
    salt
    4 tablespoons olive oil, plus extra for boiling
    350 g/12 oz dried Italian vermicelli, spaghettini or similar long, thin
        pasta
    freshly ground black pepper

Prepare and keep separate all the ingredients for the 'raw sauce' before cooking the pasta. You can do this long before you are ready to serve.

Slice the beans in half, then cut, diagonally, into short pieces about 15 mm/½ in long. Quarter the mushrooms and cut the Mozzarella into tiny pieces. Tear or cut the basil leaves into small pieces, then chop off and discard the parsley stems, but don't chop the sprigs.

Sacrifice a whole garlic clove for this recipe but please only use half of it, or a quarter if the clove is large. Raw garlic is very important to the dish's flavour, but too much will spell ruin. Cut the garlic into tiny – but *tiny* – pieces. Chop the tomato flesh into small pieces and drain on kitchen paper.

When almost ready to serve bring a large saucepan of water to the boil. Add about 1 tablespoon salt and about 2 teaspoons olive oil. When the water is boiling rapidly, add the pasta and cook only until it is *al dente* – tender but firm to the bite, though I usually test it between my thumb and index fingernail. Dried vermicelli normally takes 5–6 minutes and spaghettini, which is a little thicker, 7–8 minutes. Dried spaghetti will need almost 10 minutes, but the dish will lose its delicate looks, though not its knock-out flavour. Fresh pasta cooks in a fraction of the time, about 2–4 minutes.

Drain the pasta, then transfer to a warmed bowl. Quickly add the olive oil and toss it gently through the pasta to coat evenly. Season with black pepper, then toss in the prepared 'sauce' ingredients and serve *presto*!

GARLIC, PEPPER AND WALNUT PASTA

This is a terrific flavour combination to throw onto pasta for a quick meal. Variations on this last-minute, low-fat pleaser are legion.

15 minutes

Serves 4
   salt and olive oil for the water
   350 g/12 oz tagliatelle, or other dried pasta noodles
   4 tablespoons olive oil
   15 g/½ oz butter
   3–4 large garlic cloves, thinly sliced
   1 small red pepper, seeded and sliced into thin rings
   4 tablespoons chopped walnuts
   3–4 tablespoons freshly grated Parmesan cheese

For garnish
fresh fennel, parsley sprigs or 4 cm/1½ in long, fresh chives

Bring a large saucepan of water to the boil, add lots of salt and about 1 tablespoon olive oil, then add the pasta gradually so it doesn't break the boil too much. Boil for 10 minutes, or until the pasta is tender but slightly resilient to the bite.

Meanwhile, heat the oil and butter in a small pan over a medium-low heat, add the garlic and cook, stirring occasionally, until it begins to brown. Add the pepper rings and stir the mixture for about 30 seconds, stir in the chopped walnuts and remove the pan from the heat.

Drain the pasta and transfer to a large warmed serving bowl. Reheat the garlic mixture briefly and add it, and most of the cheese, to the pasta and toss well. Sprinkle over the rest of the cheese and your garnish.

- It's a long shot that any of us will have fennel sprigs on hand when throwing together this sort of repast, but the pretty green sprigs cut from the top of bulb fennel really do add unexpected aplomb, and a fresh, crisp texture to an already delightful dish.

NOODLES WITH BASIL SAUCE, PINE NUTS AND MANGO

The clever juxtaposition of flavours, and ingredients on the plate, can create an outstandingly simple but beautiful dish. This is one of them, perfect as an elegant starter, lunch or supper dish. Tagliatelle verde, made green with the addition of spinach, and sold dried, is particularly pretty to use here.

30 minutes

Serves 4–6
about 25 fresh basil leaves
175 g/6 oz plain, Greek-style yoghurt
a very little freshly squeezed lemon juice (optional)
50 g/2 oz pine nuts
1 tablespoon salt
1 tablespoon olive oil
350 g/12 oz dried tagliatelle, preferably green
coarsely ground black pepper
1 mango, cut into 4–6 slices

Heat the grill to high. Pound the basil leaves in a pestle and mortar to make about 1 tablespoon basil purée. Mix into the yoghurt, taste and add a few drops of lemon juice if wished. Spread the pine nuts on a baking tray and toast lightly under the grill, watching constantly, then reserve them.

Bring a very large saucepan of water to the boil. Add the salt and olive oil, then add the pasta and boil for 8 minutes, or until the noodles are tender yet firm when tested. Drain quickly and put onto warmed serving plates. Spoon a wide ribbon of basil sauce over the pasta, then sprinkle the nuts across the sauce ribbon in an 'X'. Grind over black pepper and garnish each serving with a slice of mango.

- Keep basil or a mixed herb purée all winter, by picking the fresh leaves from several plants and processing them with a very little olive oil in a food processor or blender. Transfer the purée to a small, narrow jar, pushing it down the sides of the jar and covering the top with a thin layer of olive oil. Seal the jar and refrigerate, making sure to keep the top of the purée well covered with oil after taking any out to flavour sauces, omelettes or other dishes.

LOW-FAT PIZZAS

Pizza dough, frozen in one-pizza portions, is an item to have on hand, ready to defrost and bake with the toppings of your choice.

20 minutes, plus about 3¼ hours proving and rising the dough, then about 15–20 minutes topping and baking

Makes 6 × 20–23 cm/8–9 in pizza bases
  1 tablespoon dried yeast, or 40 g/1½ oz fresh yeast (see below)
  pinch of sugar
  800 g/1¾ lb plain flour
  1 teaspoon salt

Crumble the fresh yeast, or stir the dried yeast, into 125 ml/4 fl oz lukewarm water with the sugar, and set it aside for 10–15 minutes to let it become frothy, or prove. (If using Easy Blend yeast, see below.) Meanwhile, sift the flour with the salt onto a large work surface and make a well in the centre. Pour in the yeast liquid and work in the flour gradually from the sides. Add about 225 ml/8 fl oz warm water as necessary so you can form a slightly sticky ball. Or, if you prefer, use a food processor, and sift the flour and salt into the container fitted with the metal blade. Start the machine and slowly pour in the yeast mixture, then the warm water. Process until the dough forms one mass. Remove the dough from the container.

With the base of your palm, knead the dough, adding a little more warm water if the dough is dry or crumbly. Continue kneading the dough until it becomes smooth and elastic, about 10 minutes in all, to eliminate the extra gas produced by the yeast. Divide into six equal pieces, placing them *well* apart on a lightly floured surface in a warm, draught-free place. Cover with a floured cloth and let them rise until doubled in size, about 3 hours.

Punch each portion down and briefly knead until it can be rolled into a circle. If you are not going to use the dough right away, roll into balls, wrap each one generously in cling film and refrigerate in an airtight container for 3–4 days. Or, wrap in cling film, put in a plastic bag or other container and freeze for up to 2 months. Let the dough come to room temperature and knead briefly before rolling it out. If you're planning a party, or become a pizza fanatic, make the dough in double batches.

Each portion of dough will make a pizza 20–23 cm/8–9 in in diameter and about 3–4 mm/⅛–¼ in thick. A good trick is to roll each base out to about half its eventual size, place it on a lightly oiled baking sheet, or pizza pan, then push it with your fingers to its final size. If the topping is going to be rather wet, perhaps, say, with plenty of tomato sauce, push the dough from the centre towards the edge to make a slightly higher outside crust.

When you add the topping, leave a narrow border, about 15 mm/ ½ in, around the edge as the uncovered dough will puff up during baking to form a low crust. The toppings should just cover the base and rarely be thicker than the base itself. A thick pile of ingredients tends to burn while the base becomes soggy, and too little topping cooks quickly and can lead to a dry or burnt, dull pizza.

Good pizza must be cooked at a high temperature, in an oven preheated to 220°C/425°F/gas 7. It is done when the edges are golden brown, about 10–20 minutes.

Low-fat pizza toppings

Pizzas can be low-fat as well as festive, provided high-fat cheeses, salami sausages or cured fatty ham (such as Italian *pancetto*) are not used in the toppings. The little olive oil, Parmesan cheese and herbs used on most pizzas are fine, but we can be creative choosing other ingredients according to what's available in the larder or market, be they vegetables, fruit, fish, meat or poultry.

Below are a few of my favourite toppings which may inspire you to create your own combinations. Each one is for a 20–23 cm/8–9 in pizza base. Be sure the oven is preheated to 220°C/425°F/gas 7.

- Spread 4 tablespoons tomato sauce (pages 166–7) or packaged strained, crushed tomatoes (available in many delicatessens) over the base almost to the edge and sprinkle over 1 small, thinly sliced onion, divided into rings, 1½ teaspoons oregano, 1 canned, drained and thinly sliced artichoke heart and a few pine nuts. Sprinkle on some black pepper, 2–3 tablespoons Parmesan cheese, 1 tablespoon olive oil, then bake.
- Dribble 1 tablespoon olive oil over the base almost to the edge and scatter on 50–75 g/2–3 oz wiped and finely sliced button mushrooms. Dribble over another tablespoon of olive oil, sprinkle with Parmesan cheese and bake.
- Spread about 125 g/4 oz Ricotta cheese (if it is very fresh) or crumble it over the base, then scatter on 2 cored, peeled and finely chopped apples. Sprinkle with 1 tablespoon olive oil and bake.
- Scatter over 50–75 g/2–3 oz drained, flaked tuna fish (canned in water), then cover with 1 small, preferably red, onion or 2–3 shallots, thinly sliced and divided into rings. Sprinkle on 2–3 tablespoons Parmesan cheese and 1 tablespoon olive oil, then bake.
- Romano cheese is another of Italy's low-fat triumphs, and delicious when used in place of Parmesan. However, a whole new flavour is created when you combine grated Romano and Parmesan in equal parts. Dribble 1 tablespoon olive oil over a pizza base, then scatter on 2 tablespoons each of the cheeses. Sprinkle on another tablespoon of oil and bake.
- Scatter 125 g/4 oz drained, bottled or canned tiny clams over the pizza base, grind over some black pepper, then sprinkle with 1½ teaspoons oregano and 2–3 tablespoons Parmesan or Romano cheese, and bake.
- Spread 4 tablespoons tomato sauce (pages 166–7) or packaged strained, crushed tomatoes almost to the edge of the pizza, then crumble on about 125 g/4 oz leftover meatloaf. Sprinkle with a finely chopped garlic clove, 2–3 tablespoons finely chopped onion or spring onions, and 1–2 teaspoons olive oil, then bake.
- Brush 1 tablespoon olive oil over the base almost to the edge, then scatter over 2 teaspoons dry-roasted or grilled sesame seeds. Crumble on 50–75 g/2–3 oz Ricotta cheese, and dribble over another tablespoon olive oil, then bake.

CORN BREAD WITH RUM-SOAKED RAISINS

My grandmother's corn bread is the first bread I can remember eating and, to me, it's more satisfying than white, brown, granary or other yeast-risen loaves. My corn bread is simple to make, so moist it keeps well, covered, for 3 days or so and is absolutely delicious to eat at any time – without butter. For parties, I make several loaves to serve sliced with tripe avocado, low-fat soured cream (page 42) and/or chilli jam (page 41). For breakfast it's delicious with apricot or plum jam, or you can crumble it and use in poultry stuffings as fresh breadcrumbs. Buy the corn meal, sometimes called maize meal, at whole- or healthfood stores.

Corn bread is good with plain raisins or without raisins at all. Rum-soaked raisins are an aberration from my teetotal grandma's original version, but they certainly are a fine and quite chic complement to the bread's rich savoury flavour, and its pretty yellow colour.

about 30 minutes

Makes 1 × 700 g/1½ lb loaf
  150 g/5 oz yellow corn meal or maize meal
  125 g/4 oz plain flour
  1½ teaspoons baking powder
  ½ teaspoon bicarbonate of soda
  2 teaspoons sugar (optional)
  1 teaspoon salt
  400 g/14 oz plain, Greek-style yoghurt
  2 large egg whites
  4–5 tablespoons rum-soaked raisins (see below), drained
  1 tablespoon melted butter, for greasing

Heat the oven to 220°C/425°F/gas 7. Thoroughly mix the corn meal, flour, baking powder, bicarbonate of soda, sugar if using, and salt. In another bowl whisk together the yoghurt and egg whites, then mix quickly, with just a few strokes, into the corn meal. Fold in the raisins.

Pour the melted butter into a 900 g/2 lb loaf tin and tilt it to cover the bottom well and three-quarters of the way up the sides. Spoon in the corn bread mixture and bake for about 20 minutes, or until the top is risen, firm and just beginning to brown. Let the bread cool about 5 minutes before removing from the tin, then cut into the loaf and immediately enjoy the first warm slice.

- To make rum-soaked raisins, pack a small preserving jar with raisins, then fill to the top with dark rum. Seal the jar, so it's quite airtight, and leave for about 24 hours. Top the jar up with more rum, reseal and keep for corn bread, desserts, stuffings, when you've been a good child . . .

LOW-FAT CROÛTONS

Giving up croûtons on my low-fat regime was depressing. Most of them, homemade or otherwise, are sautéed in an ocean of flavoured butter, which they soak up like sponges, before being baked to crisp them. Here, you crisp them first, sauté them in a tiny bit of oil, then toss them in herbs and grated hard cheese.

3–4 days staling the bread, then 15 minutes

Makes 225 g/8 oz (about 60 large) croûtons
    450 g/1 lb loaf unsliced white bread, left to stale for 3–4 days
    6 tablespoons olive or other polyunsaturated oil
    4 tablespoons freshly grated Parmesan, Romano or similar hard
       cheese (optional)
    4 teaspoons dried thyme, marjoram, chervil, oregano etc.

Heat the oven to 180°C/350°F/gas 4. Cut away the crusts, to give a rectangular loaf, then cut, lengthways, into four even slices. Keeping the slices together, turn the loaf onto its side, and again cut lengthways into four. You should now have sixteen long batons of bread. Holding as many together as possible, again cut into four – to give you sixty-four large cubes! Spread the bread over a baking tray and crisp in the oven for 8–10 minutes.
    Heat half the oil in a large frying pan over a medium-low heat. Add the crisped bread, stir slowly with a wooden spoon for about 2 minutes, then slowly dribble over the remaining oil as you continue to stir. Transfer the croûtons to a large bowl and sprinkle over the cheese, if using, then the dried thyme, stirring to coat well. Leave to cool.
    Store the croûtons in an airtight container for up to 3 days or freeze for up to 3 months.

- Often I divide the croûtons into batches and toss each batch in a different flavouring before freezing them separately.

DESSERTS

JUICY FRESH FRUIT SALAD

CHOCOLATE-RICOTTA CHEESECAKE

PEARS POACHED IN MAPLE SYRUP

BANANA AND CHESTNUT PARCELS

LOW-FAT CHOCOLATE MOCHA CAKE

MOCHA ICING
Mocha-rum icing

SUMMER PUDDING

CHOCOLATE-ALMOND MOUSSE
Chocolate-coffee-brandy mousse
Chocolate orange mousse

STRAWBERRY SORBET, WITH ORANGE
Strawberry sorbet, with kirsch
Raspberry sorbet, with kirsch
Blackcurrant sorbet, with gin
Blackcurrant sorbet and vanilla ice cream, with crème de cassis

GOOSEBERRY FOOL
Gooseberry fool, with dessert gooseberries
Gooseberry fool, frozen

PEACHES IN WHITE WINE
Peaches in white wine, with sorbet

CINNAMON-RHUBARB MOUSSE

RASPBERRY FOOL
Raspberry fool, frozen
Strawberry fool
Strawberry fool, frozen

CANTALOUPE WITH CARAWAY AND GIN

ORANGE-CARDAMOM FANTASY

CALYPSO SEDUCTION

RHUBARB-CHEESE FOOL

PEACHES AND CREAM

Fats I can decline; puddings I cannot. Nor can most people, which is why I have included a succulent selection in this chapter. Many of the desserts use fresh fruit, but there is also a delicious low-fat chocolate cake, cheesecake and mousse.

A number of traditional desserts are made with pastry. These I avoid, since nearly 50 per cent of the pastry is fat, and that makes me ill. If you are keen on admittedly wonderful desserts such as apple pie or black-berry crumble, enjoy them as an occasional indulgence, but consider baking pies in a deep dish with only a top crust, and using a polyunsaturated soft margarine to make the pastry or crumble. The result may not be quite up to your mother's standard, but it will be better for you.

Thick, rich cream poured over, or used in, many traditional desserts is another hurdle to scoot round, and here I use plain, Greek-style yoghurt, sweetened with icing sugar. I prefer it – and living longer – to cream, and so may you.

JUICY FRESH FRUIT SALAD

Many people love fruit salad as a refreshing, light finish to a meal. It was never a favourite with me as the fruit tended to be dry, unless it was soaked in a sugary syrup and that masked the taste of the fruit. But now it's possible to add packaged fresh juice instead of syrup, so everyone – including me – wants seconds.

Ingredients for a fresh fruit salad are a matter of preference, and seasonal availability. Peaches, strawberries and other soft fruit make wonderful additions. Here is a basic recipe for you to enjoy, and to which you can add. If you prefer a sweeter salad, mix or substitute the orange juice with mango or mixed tropical juices, peach nectar or another similar juice. Make the salad ahead of time and refrigerate to let the flavours blend.

15 minutes

Serves 4–6
    2 medium-sized red apples
    2 medium-sized yellow apples
    425–575 ml/¾–1 pint packaged fresh orange juice
    1 large orange or grapefruit
    125–225 g/4–8 oz grapes
    1 large banana

Fruit salads should be colourful and look bold, I think. This also has the advantage of reducing the amount of preparation involved. For instance, chop the apples into quarters, slice away the core and cut each quarter in half lengthways, then put in a deep bowl or dish. Cover with some of the orange juice to stop discolouration.

Slice off the top and bottom of the orange or grapefruit and turn the fruit on a cut side. Slice downwards with a sharp knife against the fruit, angling the knife as you cut, to remove the peel and pith. Hold the orange over the bowl or dish and make 'V' cuts between the membranes to remove the segments. Add them to the bowl, then squeeze the juice from the membrane over the fruit before discarding it.

Halve and seed the grapes and add them to the dish. Peel the banana, cut it across into thick rounds and stir into the salad, together with the remaining juice. Leave, if possible, for 2–4 hours in the refrigerator. Soft fruit such as bananas will macerate in the juice, adding a richness to the flavour.

- In summer I open-freeze red and blackcurrants, then bag and store them in the freezer. A few of the colourful berries sprinkled into a winter fruit salad gives an extra sparkle.

CHOCOLATE-RICOTTA CHEESECAKE

Rich in texture and flavour but low in fat, this airy-light cheesecake is a marvellous finale to a good meal, when guests insist they couldn't swallow another mouthful. But they will. Then they'll ask for the recipe.

40 minutes

Serves 4–6
  unsalted butter, for greasing
  125 g/4 oz finest plain chocolate
  450 g/1 lb Ricotta cheese
  pinch of salt (optional)
  1 tablespoon flour
  125 g/4 oz soft brown sugar
  2 medium-sized egg yolks
  1 teaspoon finely grated orange zest
  3 medium-sized egg whites
  2 tablespoons icing sugar

Heat the oven to 190°C/375°F/gas 5. Butter an 850 ml/1½ pint soufflé dish and set aside. Melt the chocolate in the top of a double boiler over gently simmering water. Mix together the melted chocolate, Ricotta, salt, if using, flour, brown sugar, egg yolks and orange zest.

Whisk the egg whites until stiff but not dry. With a hand whisk, stir one-third of them into the cheese mixture to lighten it, then fold in the remaining whites quickly. Pour the mixture into the soufflé dish and bake in the centre of the oven for 25 minutes or until it is well risen and feels firm when lightly touched on top. Sift over the icing sugar and serve immediately.

- Unlike proper soufflés, this dish does not suffer gastronomically if it is eaten warm, though it does lose a little height.

PEARS POACHED IN MAPLE SYRUP

The combination of pears and maple syrup is light and welcome at the
end of a meal; the filling is a nice surprise.

45 minutes–1¼ hours, plus chilling

Serves 6
    6 large ripe, but firm, pears without any blemishes
    275 ml/½ pint pure maple syrup
    175 g/6 oz Ricotta cheese
    125 g/4 oz walnuts, chopped

    For serving
    6–12 tablespoons maple syrup

With a 9 cm/3½ in long apple corer or, failing this, a thin potato peeler,
carefully core the pears from the bottom end, leaving the stems and peel
intact. Trim the bottoms so the pears stand upright.

Pour the maple syrup into a small saucepan with an equal volume of
water and bring almost to the boil. Lower the heat, and gently simmer
the pears, one at a time, until tender but not too soft, 5–10 minutes.
Stand each pear upright to drain and cool, adding more water as
necessary to poach the other pears. Cool, then refrigerate the syrup to
use again.

With a very sharp, small knife, carefully peel each pear downwards,
starting near, but not at, the stem. Mix the cheese and nuts together,
then carefully fill the pears with the mixture, pushing it in with the
handle of a teaspoon. Stand the pears on a plate, cover loosely with cling
film and refrigerate.

Drizzle 1–2 tablespoons maple syrup (not the poaching liquid) over
each chilled pear before serving.

BANANA AND CHESTNUT PARCELS

A warm dessert – delicious to eat and easy to make.

30 minutes

Serves 4
  4–6 medium-sized firm ripe bananas
  175 g/6 oz *marrons glacés* in syrup (5–6 whole *marrons glacés*),
    chopped
  25 g/1 oz butter, cut into small pieces

Heat the oven to 140°C/275°F/gas 1. Peel the bananas and cut into
20 mm/¾ in thick slices. Arrange the slices on a piece of foil about
28 cm/11 in square, sprinkle over the chopped *marrons glacés*, dot with
the butter, then fold up the ends of the foil into a parcel. Place on a
baking tray in the oven and cook for 25 minutes.
  Transfer the parcel to a plate, and serve, opening it at the table.

• For a quicker dessert, cook for 10 minutes at 180°C/350°F/gas 4.
• For individual parcels, divide the fruit between 4 × 20 cm/8 in squares of
  foil, bake, then serve on individual plates, from the parcels.

LOW-FAT CHOCOLATE MOCHA CAKE

Maybe it was my misspent youth, maybe my mother's delight in serving
rich chocolate cake for breakfast, but I still lust for chocolate cake, at
any hour. So I concocted my own cake – dark, moist, intense in
flavour, and low in fat.

about 1¼ hours, plus cooling

Serves 8–10
  75 g/3 oz unsalted butter, plus extra for greasing
  175 g/6 oz flour, plus extra for dusting
  350 g/12 oz sugar
  3 large egg whites
  ½–¾ teaspoon vanilla essence
  50 g/2 oz cocoa
  ⅜ teaspoon bicarbonate of soda
  ⅜ teaspoon baking powder
  4 tablespoons instant coffee powder
  125 ml/4 fl oz skimmed milk
  pinch of salt (optional)

Grease and flour a 900 g/2 lb loaf tin. Heat the oven to 180°C/350°F/gas 4.

Meanwhile, cream the butter and sugar together with an electric whisk, then whisk in the egg whites until the mixture is very thick. Add the vanilla essence and set aside.

Sift together the flour, cocoa, bicarbonate of soda and baking powder and reserve. Mix 125 ml/4 fl oz boiling water into the instant coffee powder and pour in the milk. Whisk one-third of the flour into the egg-white mixture, then add one-third of the coffee, beating well in. Add half the remaining flour, whisk well, then half the coffee, again mixing well. Beat in the rest of the flour, then coffee, blending very thoroughly. Taste and add salt if wished.

Pour into the prepared tin and bake about 50 minutes, or until the cake is done when tested with a skewer. Cool it in the tin for 20–30 minutes before turning out onto a wire rack to finish cooling. Store in an airtight container.

MOCHA ICING

I am happy to eat my chocolate cake without icing, but for special occasions, try it with this chocolate mocha coating.

10 minutes

Ices a 900 g/2 lb cake
    25 g/1 oz plain chocolate
    25 g/1 oz cocoa
    25 g/1 oz unsalted butter
    2 tablespoons instant coffee powder
    400 g/14 oz icing sugar
    2–3 teaspoons ground cinnamon
    ½–¾ teaspoon vanilla essence

For garnish
chopped pistachios, or flaked, toasted almonds

Melt the chocolate in a double boiler or in a bowl over a pan of simmering water. Then, in a food processor, or with an electric whisk, beat together the melted chocolate, cocoa and butter. Dissolve the coffee in 6 tablespoons boiling water, then whisk into the chocolate.

Add the icing sugar, cinnamon and vanilla essence. If too thick, process in 1–2 teaspoonfuls hot water; if too thin, add another 2–3 tablespoons icing sugar.

Cut the cold cake in half, putting the top layer upside-down on a serving plate. Spread the icing lightly around the sides then over the top. Cover with the second layer, smoothest side uppermost, and repeat. Scatter over chopped pistachios or flaked, toasted almonds to decorate.

- For a mocha-rum icing, omit the cinnamon and vanilla, reduce the boiling water to 4 tablespoons and add 1½ tablespoons dark rum.

SUMMER PUDDING

Simple, but one of the year's most exquisite puddings. Try my favourite version in fine low-fat, if not traditional English style with sweetened thick yoghurt.

40 minutes, plus overnight chilling

Serves 6–8
    225 g/8 oz redcurrants, stalks removed
    225 g/8 oz sugar
    2 tablespoons orange juice
    225 g/8 oz loganberries, hulled
    225 g/8 oz raspberries, hulled
    8–10 thin slices of white bread, crusts removed
    225–350 g/8–12 oz strawberries, hulled
    grenadine syrup (optional)
    2–3 tablespoons icing sugar, sifted
    about 450 ml/1 lb plain, Greek-style yoghurt

Put the currants in a heavy-based saucepan over a medium heat. Sprinkle over the sugar and add the orange juice. When the mixture begins to bubble, cover the pan and cook over a very low heat for about 5 minutes, shaking the pan occasionally, until the juices flow and the sugar dissolves.

Add the loganberries and raspberries to the pan, cover and continue cooking for 3 minutes. Remove the lid, take the pan off the heat and let the mixture cool.

Meanwhile, line the bottom and sides of a 1.1 litre/2 pint pudding basin with most of the bread, cutting so that it fits in neatly, and patching any holes with the trimmings.

Stir the strawberries into the cooled fruit mixture and reserve 75 ml/3 fl oz of the liquid. Pour the rest of the mixture into the lined bowl, then cover the top completely with more bread.

Place a small plate on top of the bowl fitting it, if possible, just inside the rim, then weight the top. Chill overnight.

Just before serving, run a table knife around the inside rim of the bowl to loosen the bread. Place a serving plate upside-down over the basin, then quickly invert the two. Remove the basin and spoon over the reserved juice onto any white, unsoaked areas of bread. Add a sprinkling of grenadine syrup as well, if wished (see below).

Sift icing sugar onto the yoghurt, stir it gently in and serve with the summer pudding.

- Far too short is the season for this favourite dessert, so I often increase the quantities of the fruit mixture when making my summer pudding, for freezing. Line aluminium freezer storage containers, individual portion size, with bread and proceed as above. The next day, cover each container with foil and freeze upright.
- In November, February or whenever I decide to serve my summer pudding, and there is no reserved liquid to soak any white spots, I sprinkle over grenadine syrup. It works so well that I sometimes also add the syrup to my 'summer' summer puddings!

CHOCOLATE-ALMOND MOUSSE

Sublime is the aptest description for this dessert. Traditional, ultra-thick, rich-with-egg-yolks, chocolate mousse has its place – on the way to cholesterol suicide – but here is a truly glorious and healthy alternative. The finer the chocolate used, the better the mousse.

30 minutes, plus chilling

Serves 6
100–175 g/4–6 oz best plain chocolate, cut into small pieces
275 g/10 oz silken tofu
3 tablespoons almond liqueur
about 3 tablespoons icing sugar
3 large egg whites

For garnish
3–4 tablespoons flaked almonds (optional)

Melt the chocolate in a double boiler, or in a bowl over a pan of barely simmering water. Meanwhile, drain the tofu and squeeze it in a tea cloth to remove excess water. You'll be left with about 150 g/5 oz of tofu, once drained.

Put the melted chocolate, tofu, almond liqueur and icing sugar into a blender or food processor and blend until smooth. Taste the mixture and add more sugar and liqueur if wished, then transfer to a large bowl.

Whisk the egg whites until they hold soft peaks, then whisk one-third into the chocolate mixture to distribute thoroughly. Lightly fold in the rest of the whites and divide the mousse between wine glasses or small serving bowls. Refrigerate six hours or overnight to allow the flavours to develop.

An hour or so before serving, spread the flaked almonds, if using, over a baking tray and toast under a hot grill for 1–2 minutes, watching carefully to prevent scorching. Let them cool, then scatter the nuts over the mousse before serving.

- For a chocolate-coffee-brandy mousse, soak 4 plain tea biscuits or macaroons in 2½ tablespoons brandy, then purée in a food processor with 175 g/6 oz best plain melted chocolate, 175 ml/3 fl oz freshly made, cooled strong black coffee and the silken tofu, prepared as above. Fold in 3 large egg whites and chill.

- For chocolate orange mousse use orange liqueur instead of almond liqueur.

STRAWBERRY SORBET, WITH ORANGE

Lusciously textured, gloriously flavoured, fresh fruit sorbets are delightful at any time and a dream for dinner parties. Even without a sorbetière, they are SIMPLE to make, so overcome your reluctance, enjoy a new category of no-fat homemade treats and boost your cook's confidence at the same time.

25 minutes, plus 5–6 hours freezing

Serves 4
450 g/1 lb ripe, firm strawberries, hulled
1 tablespoon Cointreau, triple sec, or other orange-flavoured liqueur

1 tablespoon powdered gelatine
175 g/6 oz sugar
1 large egg white

Two hours ahead, turn the freezer to its lowest temperature. Purée the strawberries in a food processor or, in batches, in a blender. Transfer to a bowl and stir in the liqueur.

Put 4 tablespoons cold water into a small bowl, sprinkle over the gelatine and leave for 5 minutes. Meanwhile, put the sugar and 225 ml/8 fl oz water in a saucepan over a medium heat and stir until the sugar dissolves. Bring the mixture to the boil, then simmer for 4–5 minutes. Remove the syrup from the heat, stir in the softened gelatine and leave the syrup to cool, 10–15 minutes.

Stir the syrup into the fruit purée, pour the mixture into a large shallow plastic or metal container that will fit easily into the freezer, then freeze for about 45 minutes or until the edges of the mixture begin to freeze. Remove the container and stir the mixture vigorously with a hand whisk. Repeat this 3–4 times, over about 2 hours, or until the sorbet is very thick when you finish stirring it.

Beat the egg white until stiff but not dry, then stir thoroughly through the sorbet. Replace the container and freeze for a further 1–2 hours, vigorously stirring the sorbet when it begins to freeze at the edges. If you like, spoon the sorbet into a pretty mould and freeze the mixture for at least 2 more hours before serving.

To serve, soften the sorbet in the refrigerator for 15 minutes before spooning it out. If using a mould, put the mould over a serving plate and wrap a towel, wrung out in very hot water, around the mould. The sorbet will plop out onto the plate. Serve immediately, cutting the sorbet with a knife dipped, between each slice, in hot water.

- Try strawberry sorbet with kirsch (cherry eau de vie) instead of orange liqueur.
- Raspberry sorbet, for my money, is a truly elegant cooler and is made as above, replacing the strawberries and orange liqueur with raspberries and kirsch, or framboise (raspberry eau de vie).
- Another crowd-pleaser is made by blending 900 g/2 lb blackcurrants, stems removed, to a purée, then sieving the purée and discarding the seeds. Instead of a fruit liqueur or brandy, flavour this with 1½ tablespoons dry gin or, for extra zing, the more pungent Dutch gin.
- If your diet will permit, or your guests seem to warrant the splurge, serve a scoop of blackcurrant sorbet with a scoop of vanilla ice cream and dribble crème de cassis over the top.

GOOSEBERRY FOOL

The tartness of gooseberries and plain yoghurt makes one of the best, if not *the* best, summer fool. I've tried making it with a mouli and a food processor; both work well, but the latter is quicker.

40 minutes–1 hour, plus chilling

Serves 4
    900 g/2 lb gooseberries, washed and drained
    175–275 g/6–10 oz sugar
    about 1 tablespoon freshly squeezed lemon juice
    350 g/12 oz plain yoghurt

Chop the fruit coarsely, sprinkle over sugar to taste and leave for 20–30 minutes.

If using a mouli, fit it with the finest blade, place the mouli over a bowl and put the gooseberries through. If using a food processor, purée the fruit, in batches if necessary, then strain the purée through a sieve.

Add lemon juice to taste, to balance the sugar, then stir in the yoghurt thoroughly. Pour the mixture into a serving bowl and chill until cold, or overnight.

- If you just miss the all too short season of tart cooking gooseberries, you can make the fool with dessert gooseberries. Just reduce the sugar accordingly.
- For frozen gooseberry fool, pour into freezer containers and freeze overnight. Twenty minutes before serving, transfer the containers to the refrigerator, to slightly soften the fool.

PEACHES IN WHITE WINE

While they are in season, a bowl of poached peaches sits in my refrigerator, their luscious goodness ready at any time for instant desserts and delightful nibbles.

20 minutes, plus cooling

Serves 6
    6 large firm, ripe peaches (about 1.4 kg/3 lb)
    1 bottle (70 cl) dry white wine

1–2 tablespoons sugar (optional)
lemon juice or vanilla essence (optional)

Halve the peaches and remove the stones. Lay the halves flat, then cut into evenly-sized slices. Put the slices in a small saucepan and cover with the wine. Bring to the boil, then simmer for about 10 minutes until tender but not too soft. Drain and return the liquid to the saucepan. Spread the peaches out on a platter, or baking tin, to cool.

Taste the liquid and add a little sugar, if wished. Simmer for 2–3 minutes, then pour the liquid into a large bowl to cool. Add a few drops of lemon juice or vanilla essence, if wished; the additions will depend on the flavour of the peaches you use. When the liquid is cool, add the fruit to the syrup and chill.

- For a special treat, serve the peaches and syrup in long-stemmed wine glasses, with a scoop of raspberry, or other, sorbet on top (pages 186-7).

CINNAMON-RHUBARB MOUSSE

Charmed by the idea, people will be knocked out by the flavour of this sublime little number.

1 hour 20 minutes, plus cooling and chilling

Serves 6–8
    350 g/12 oz rhubarb, chopped
    about 4 tablespoons soft brown sugar
    a few drops vanilla essence
    ¼ teaspoon ground cinnamon
    150 g/5 oz skimmed milk curd cheese
    1 tablespoon curaçao, or other orange-flavoured liqueur
    fresh orange juice
    1 tablespoon powdered gelatine
    2 large egg whites

Heat the oven to 140°C/275°F/gas 1. Put the rhubarb in a small ovenproof dish with the brown sugar, 175 ml/6 fl oz water and the vanilla essence, cover and place in the oven for 1 hour.

Purée the rhubarb in a food processor, or blender, with the cinnamon, cheese and liqueur, measure the purée and add orange juice or a mixture of orange juice and water to make it up to 575 ml/1 pint. Taste and stir in more brown sugar if wished. Leave to cool, stirring occasionally.

Dissolve the gelatine in 2 tablespoons warm water and leave for 5 minutes until soft, then stir into the cool rhubarb purée. Whisk the egg whites until stiff but not dry, then fold into the purée and pour the mousse into a serving dish. Cool, then refrigerate until set and serve.

- You can make up the rhubarb and cheese mixture the day or night before, then add the softened gelatine and egg whites the next day before chilling.
- And if you, quite rightly, insist on using fresh rhubarb all year, you can cook the rhubarb (when in season), with the brown sugar, water and vanilla essence, cool, divide into convenient amounts and freeze. Then you can finish the mousse any time – when the rest of us have no 'fresh' rhubarb. Or, of course, simply freeze fresh rhubarb – it's one of the best candidates for the freezer.

RASPBERRY AND STRAWBERRY FOOLS

It will occur to you that my fools are really fruit-flavoured, yoghurt mixtures. The difference is that when you make the fools yourself, you can choose the fruit you want, and use far more of it in proportion to the yoghurt than is found in the commercial brands. You can also sweeten yours – or not – according to the ripeness of the fruit, and your taste.

Choose any ripe soft fruit such as blackberries or a firmer, but very ripe fruit, such as peaches (blanched, peeled and chopped), and purée in a food processor. Mix in the sugar, then the yoghurt and refrigerate, preferably overnight, for a luscious, thick and low-fat fresh fruit fool. Here are guidelines for two.

20 minutes, plus chilling

225 g/8 oz strawberries, hulled, or raspberries
2–3 tablespoons sugar
6 tablespoons plain, Greek-style yoghurt
2–4 drops of freshly squeezed lemon juice (optional)

Purée the fruit in a food processor and sprinkle on the sugar. Stir in the yoghurt, then taste and add lemon if wished, cover and refrigerate.

- There is no reason why you shouldn't add much more yoghurt, either the Greek variety or plain, low-fat yoghurt. In the latter case, you may need to add a little more sugar.

- For a wonderfully refreshing, low-fat, iced dessert with a delightful fruity flavour, I freeze my fruit fools, soften them 20–30 minutes in the refrigerator, then spoon them into pretty dishes or glasses, and top with whole or sliced fresh fruit of the same variety.

CANTALOUPE WITH CARAWAY AND GIN

Two special desserts, this one, and the next, were given to Jack, and hence to us, by a young Australian named Stephen Baggaley. If the ingredients tempt you, then wait until you taste the dish. All resolve will be gone.

10 minutes

Serves 6
  1–2 ripe cantaloupe melons
  1 tablespoon caraway seeds
  175–350 ml/6–12 fl oz dry gin

Halve the melon, or melons, and scoop out the seeds. Slice off the ends, then cut each half, lengthways, into 4 crescent slices. Cut the flesh away from the peel, then chop into bite-sized pieces, and divide between serving dishes or goblets.

Lightly crush the caraway seeds to bring out their flavour, then put in a small saucepan with the gin. Warm the gin slightly, pour over the melon and serve at once.

ORANGE-CARDAMOM FANTASY

about 20 minutes, plus 2–4 hours macerating and chilling

Serves 6
  6–9 large oranges
  6 large cardamom pods
  225 ml/8 fl oz dry gin
  2 tablespoons freshly squeezed lemon juice
  225 g/8 oz plain, Greek-style yoghurt
  25–50 g/1–2 oz flaked almonds

Slice the ends off an orange, then stand it up on a cut end. Peel off the skin and whitish pith by 'shaving' down with a sharp knife against the flesh. Divide into segments, then chop into bite-sized pieces, removing as many seeds as possible. Or, if you wish, peel off the membranes, squeeze the juice from them, reserving the juice, discarding the membranes, then chop the flesh into cubes. Repeat with the remaining oranges. Put the oranges and juice into a bowl.

Crush the cardamom pods with the flat side of a knife and remove the small black seeds. Bruise the seeds in a pestle and mortar, then stir into the oranges with the gin and leave to macerate in the refrigerator for 2–4 hours.

Meanwhile, stir the lemon juice into the yoghurt, cover and refrigerate to let the flavour develop.

Heat the grill to high. Spread the almonds out on a baking tray and toast lightly, checking them constantly. Let the almonds cool. To serve, spoon the oranges into serving dishes or stemmed glasses, top with the yoghurt and sprinkle on the almonds.

CALYPSO SEDUCTION

'Yes, please, this is wonderful, delicious, gorgeous . . .' is the reassuring response I always get when asking if anyone would like seconds of this dessert. Reassuring because this is my quick, easy standby when I'm too disorganized – or too lazy – to prepare a more demanding sweet. But, then, I never mind a second helping of calypso seduction myself . . .

10 minutes, plus 20 minutes maceration

Serves 6
    6 large bananas
    75–125 ml/3–4 fl oz dark rum
    2–3 tablespoons icing sugar
    225 g/8 oz plain, Greek-style yoghurt
    25–50 g/1–2 oz flaked almonds

Peel the bananas and slice thinly. Put in a shallow bowl, pour over the rum and leave to macerate for at least 20 minutes, stirring occasionally.

Meanwhile, sift and stir the icing sugar into the yoghurt, cover and refrigerate. Next, heat the grill to high. Spread the almonds on a baking tray and toast lightly, stirring them once or twice. They burn in a twinkle, so watch them closely. Let the almonds cool.

When ready to serve, divide the bananas between serving plates, spoon over some of the sweetened yoghurt and sprinkle over the toasted almonds.

NB: Unless this dessert has been preceded by a vast meal, it is wise to allow for extra helpings!

RHUBARB-CHEESE FOOL

Ah, the joys of rhubarb, whether it be the delicate, pale sticks of spring or the dark red, tarter flavoured goodness of summer! Try it in this fool which has the consistency of a syllabub.

1¼ hours, plus cooling and chilling

Serves 4–6
   350 g/12 oz fresh rhubarb, chopped
   3–4 tablespoons soft brown sugar
   a few drops vanilla essence
   1½ tablespoons triple sec or other orange-flavoured liqueur
   150 g/5 oz skimmed milk soft cheese
   ¼ teaspoon ground allspice

Heat the oven to 140°C/275°F/gas 1. Put the rhubarb in a small ovenproof dish with 3 tablespoons soft brown sugar if the rhubarb is young, 4 tablespoons if it is later in the season. Add 125 ml/4 fl oz water, the vanilla essence and liqueur, cover and place in the oven for 1 hour.

Purée the rhubarb in a food processor, or blender, then briefly process or blend in the cheese and allspice. Pour the fool into a serving bowl or individual serving dishes, let it cool, then refrigerate until ready to serve.

- When the rhubarb season slips by, despair not. Use 350 g/12 oz canned, drained rhubarb puréed in a food processor, or blender, with the juice of 1 lemon and a few drops of vanilla essence. Taste and add soft brown sugar if needed and liqueur, if wished, then add the skimmed milk cheese and allspice and process briefly to mix. Pour into dishes and refrigerate as above.

PEACHES AND CREAM

Peaches and cream were synonymous with me – until my fat intake had to be drastically reduced. So delight knew no bounds when I discovered a healthy and, truly even more delicious, alternative, which can replace pouring cream in any fruit or dessert dish.

5–10 minutes

Serves 4
    2–3 tablespoons icing sugar
    225 g/8 oz plain, Greek-style yoghurt
    4 large ripe peaches, sliced

Sift the icing sugar into the yoghurt and stir well. Spoon the 'cream' over the peaches and serve.

- The sweetened yoghurt keeps well, covered, in the refrigerator for 2–3 days.

INDEX